PRAISE FOR *ARAB SPRING DREAMS*

"You are now holding an exceptional book. It ___ eyes of the whole world are anxiously set on th___ gerly looking forward to getting to know the st___ themselves heard among the brouhaha in the media. The essays collected here are a particularly important testimony and close to my heart as they are written by young courageous people who dare to dream of the things their parents never dreamt of. The book clearly demonstrates that no matter where we live or what religion we follow, certain fundamental values are universal."

—Lech Walesa, Nobel Peace Prize recipient
and the former president of Poland

"Immediate and raw, the essays in this collection provide glimpses of daily life in countries where civil rights do not exist. Though the essay contest seemed like a quixotic gesture at its inception in 2005, it turns out to have been prescient."

—*Publishers Weekly*

"For too long, American readers have looked to unreliable intermediaries to learn what's on the minds of the Arab youth. But now two of the most promising young thinkers from the region have offered up a gem, *Arab Spring Dreams*, giving us access to their generation's most authentic voices. To further their worthy fight for freedom, let us begin by lending an ear to their moving narratives."

—Roya Hakakian, author of
Journey from the Land of No and
Assassins of the Turquoise Palace

"These are extraordinary and ordinary stories that underline an immutable truth: people want to live as free beings with dignity and equal rights. This collection of powerful testimonies is gripping, heart-breaking, and inspiring, offering the only antidote to the abyss of a society lacking rule of law: educated hope. These pages reveal that the struggle for civil rights in the Middle East is still ongoing—and will require allies the world over who recognize the universality of the struggle for human rights and the responsibility borne by those of us living in freedom."

—Thor Halvorssen, President, Human Rights Foundation

"*Arab Spring Dreams* offers a compelling journey through the hearts, minds, and souls of the generation that rocked the world's most repressive region. A firsthand account of the struggle for democracy in the Middle East and a terrific roller coaster of burning frustrations and passionate aspirations. Buckle up!"

—Ahmed Benchemsi, Stanford University Center on Democracy, Development and the Rule of Law

"This book inspires hope that today's younger generations of Arabs and Iranians will bequeath to their children a much more tolerant and democratic Middle East than the one they inherited from their parents."

—Karim Sadjadpour, Carnegie Endowment for International Peace

"Sohrab Ahmari and Nasser Weddady have assembled a chorus of new voices from across the Arab and Iranian Middle East, and all of the voices are young, and all of them are plaintive. Not everyone among the contributors to this anthology sees things the same way, but everyone is filled with yearning for a better future, and the yearning is touching. Will the better future come about? One thing is certain: a better future for the Middle East and for the larger world will come about only if people from different corners of the world do a better job of speaking to one another. *Arab Spring Dreams* contributes to that noble cause. And Ahmari and Weddady are writers to watch."

—Paul Berman, author of *Terror and Liberalism*
and *The Flight of the Intellectuals*

ARAB SPRING DREAMS

ARAB SPRING DREAMS

THE NEXT GENERATION SPEAKS OUT FOR FREEDOM AND JUSTICE FROM NORTH AFRICA TO IRAN

EDITED BY NASSER WEDDADY AND SOHRAB AHMARI

FOREWORD BY GLORIA STEINEM

FEATURING WRITINGS FROM THE AMERICAN ISLAMIC CONGRESS'S DREAM DEFERRED ESSAY CONTEST

palgrave
macmillan

ARAB SPRING DREAMS
Copyright © American Islamic Congress, 2012.
All rights reserved.

First published in 2012 by PALGRAVE MACMILLAN® in the U.S.—a division
of St. Martin's Press LLC, 175 Fifth Avenue, New York, NY 10010.

Where this book is distributed in the UK, Europe and the rest of the world, this
is by Palgrave Macmillan, a division of Macmillan Publishers Limited, registered
in England, company number 785998, of Houndmills, Basingstoke, Hampshire
RG21 6XS.

Palgrave Macmillan is the global academic imprint of the above companies and
has companies and representatives throughout the world.

Palgrave® and Macmillan® are registered trademarks in the United States, the
United Kingdom, Europe and other countries.

ISBN: 978-0-230-11592-7

Library of Congress Cataloging-in-Publication Data

Arab spring dreams : the next generation speaks out for freedom and justice from
North Africa to Iran / edited by Sohrab Ahmari and Nasser Weddady ; foreword
by Gloria Steinem.
    p.   cm.
  Includes index.
  ISBN 978-0-230-11592-7 (pbk.)
    1. Youth—Middle East—Social conditions.   2. Youth—Political activity—
Middle East.   3. Youth movements—Middle East.   4. Youth—Middle
East—Biography.   5. Civil rights—Middle East.   6. Middle East—Politics
and government—21st century.   7. Middle East—Social conditions—21st
century.   I. Ahmari, Sohrab.   II. Weddady, Nasser.
HQ799.M628A73   2012
305.2350956—dc23

                                                              2011040448

A catalogue record of the book is available from the British Library.

Design by Letra Libre, Inc.

First edition: May 2012
10 9 8 7 6 5 4 3 2 1

Printed in the United States of America.

CONTENTS

To the thousands of young Middle Easterners who have shared their dreams with us—and to Jesse Sage, mentor, friend, dreamer.

To my late brother Wael, whose birth I missed, and whose funeral I could not attend.

—Nasser Weddady

To my mother.

—Sohrab Ahmari

FOREWORD
THE POWER OF STORIES

Gloria Steinem

FOR MOST OF HUMAN HISTORY, WE HAVE BEEN GATHERING around campfires for light and warmth and telling stories.

This is the way our history came down to us and also came to include us. This is the way a woman or a man or a child told us what happened to them that day. This is the way one person told of a danger or heard others who experienced it, too, and all could discover that it was not a personal weakness, or that in the telling, there was a shared solution.

Symptoms of illness were recognized in stories, humor was turned into group laughter, and a person with a gift for predicting the weather could share it. So could someone who found a school of fish or a faraway trove of berries or the handprints and drawings left in caves or on rock faces by other groups as symbols of their stories.

Telling stories meant sitting in a circle while one person at a time spoke and others listened. Often there was a symbolic object that was passed to each in turn. Only he or she could speak while holding it. Since each had to be listened to, there was a natural rhythm of stories that were short or long, a democracy of speaking and listening.

A parent or an elder might tell a child's story before she or he had language to speak, and observe the unique person within that child. Indeed, uniqueness was often the source of a child's naming. Later, speech continued that unique story in the child's own words, and she or he joined the circle, too.

If there was a decision that involved more than one such group—say, the fate of a water hole or the use of a migratory path—each group selected a Wise Person to sit in a circle with those from other groups. This was the beginning of governance with the collective welfare in mind.

Some form of this sequence of circles was known to the original cultures of southern and eastern Africa where all humans originated, and spread with them along migratory paths to southern India and Australia and the Americas. The United States has only recently begun to acknowledge that the original cultures conquered by Europeans were more the source of democracy than was Greece, with its slavery and exclusion of women. The Iroquois Confederacy, a coalition of seven large and far-flung language groups, had a well-developed form of governance that balanced local with overall powers. It was imitated by the US Constitution—so much so that two Iroquois elders attended its drafting as advisors.

One question from those Iroquois was, "Where are the women?" My country took two more centuries before, as among the Iroquois, women as well as men were included in decision making and there was no slavery. We have yet to adopt the Iroquois standard of measuring each decision against the welfare of seven generations forward. But much that readers who come to this book out of interest in democracy might find positive—if still very imperfect in the United States—was developed during the first 95 percent of human history.

Now we know that only in recent millennia in some parts of the world—and only in recent centuries in others—has the paradigm of the circle changed to the pyramid or hierarchy, with those on top telling their stories while those in the middle and at the bottom only listen. I say this not to suggest answers, but to open questions:

Why is it that wherever I have witnessed original cultures as they struggle to survive or return, the way of saying someone is ill or suffering is, "She has lost her story?" Or perhaps, "He has lost his song?"

Why is it that some or many language groups—from the Dalits of India to the Cherokees of my country and the Kwei or San of the Kalahari—rarely have gendered pronouns, even though they may have many nuanced words for kinship and variations in the natural world? (I have been alternating genders in pronouns as a poor imitation of those original languages. In Romance and Germanic languages, even tables and chairs are divided by gender.)

Why is it that the oldest cultures so rarely create a hierarchy by separating "masculine" from "feminine," mind from body, intellect from emotion, humans from nature?

Perhaps the invention of gender may be the first step in suppressing some stories by dividing human beings into subject and object, active and passive, speaker and listener. Certainly, dividing humanity into "masculine" and "feminine" within our own loved family increases the likelihood that we will accept power based on race and class and ethnicity outside the family. The idea that some are born to speak and others to listen is normalized. It feels like home.

To break the cycle, it doesn't matter where you begin. You may ask those who have not spoken to tell their stories—and perform the revolutionary act of listening. You may tell your own untold story—and discover it's worth listening to. In either case, you are beginning the path back to the original democracy of the circle.

This collection of brave and honest voices from the Middle East will inspire you. Here, you will meet a young woman who finds herself mysteriously drawn to cars rather than dolls—and who thus challenges the suffering that comes when only the male story in her society includes mobility. You will meet a young man who discovers that a god portrayed as an all-powerful father can too easily turn into a totalitarian Big Brother. And you will hear the many voices of young people who refuse to believe that anyone's story can be heard only by giving one's life in order to call attention to it. In telling their own stories they honor the young Tunisian student who immolated himself and gave rise to the story of the Arab Spring.

I first became part of this circle several years ago when I was asked to be a judge for the inaugural edition of the "Dream Deferred" essay contest on civil rights in the Middle East. It was the contest that spurred the writing in this anthology. I agreed to serve as a judge because I wanted to hear what was being whispered in the Middle East beyond the censors' reach, in intimate conversations, and inside long-suppressed dreams. I am honored to be a listener.

I discovered captivating, original voices. One young Egyptian woman shared the civil rights struggles she knew within her own family—and declared with passion her refusal to forfeit her own rights. My judging scorecard singled out her essay. I didn't know then that the writer, Dalia Ziada, would go on to become one of the Middle East's most prominent voices for civil rights reform and women's equality—a journey recounted later in this anthology.

This is the book's power. It contains miraculous seeds from the minds and hearts of budding writers and thinkers. Their creativity stands in bold contrast to the repression surrounding them. Contained within these pages, you will find treasurers, surprises, and rewards.

Now you are invited to join the circle of this book and make your own discoveries. Read, listen, and then tell your own story. The path back to our future is one story at a time. We will empower each other.

—*Gloria Steinem*

INTRODUCTION

A NEW GENERATION OF
REFORMERS SPEAKS OUT

YOU HOLD IN YOUR HANDS THE WRITINGS OF YOUNG MIDDLE
Easterners who dared to share their long-repressed dreams of achieving individual rights, the very same youth you saw protesting in Cairo's Tahrir
Square, Tunis's Kassba, and Tehran's Azadi Square over the past two years.
For these budding thinkers—cursed to grow up under dictatorships with pervasive state security apparatuses designed to crush dissent—simply writing
down their thoughts meant risking their personal safety. As the editors who
had the privilege to assemble their dreams into an anthology, we feel obliged
to explain the inspiration behind their essays, the formal contest that solicited
them, and the editorial framing that shaped this book.

THE ROOTS OF AN EXPLOSION

Since the September 11, 2001, attacks on the World Trade Center and
the Pentagon, Americans have become painfully familiar with the devastating blasts emanating from the Mideast: suicide bombers who have claimed
thousands of lives around the world. Since then, Westerners have come to
see Middle Eastern youth as invariably chauvinistic, muzzling, and violent.
But against this nihilistic backdrop, inspiring bursts of nonviolent, popular

uprisings exploded in Iran, Tunisia, Egypt, Libya, Yemen, Syria, Bahrain, and elsewhere. The world is now witnessing the dramatic awakening of a Middle Eastern civil rights movement as it is relentlessly beamed out via social media platforms and traditional media outlets. Western publics are inspired by the heroic courage of youth who are defying tyrants, but unsure of the outcome of these momentous events.

Those accustomed to the region's repressive status quo have been caught by surprise. The sight of American journalists Anderson Cooper and Nicholas Kristof roughed up on camera by Egyptian security forces shook Americans out of the illusion of "moderate Arab regimes" that had for so long informed their thinking about the region. Meanwhile, the scenes of youth chanting "*silmiya, silmiya!*" (peaceful, peaceful!) while being shot with live ammunition by their governments shook the world out of its apathy and decade-long distrust of the region's youth.

Young Middle Easterners—typically viewed with trepidation as part of a reactionary "Arab street" or simply overlooked as masses passively acquiescing to despots—have shattered stereotypes by leading dignified struggles in the face of overwhelming repression. This anthology, compiled with a Western audience in mind, aims to open a rare window into the experiences and attitudes driving today's events and provide candid, first-person perspectives on being trapped in repressive societies while seeking to break through.

Collected over the course of half a decade, the essays in this anthology document the latent energy of today's Mideast civil rights movement as it swirled from 2005 to 2010. With the September 11 attacks and the subsequent invasions of Afghanistan and Iraq in hindsight, the young thinkers featured here began writing shortly after Lebanon's 2005 Cedar Revolution. Hundreds of thousands of young Lebanese had bravely taken to the streets in a nonviolent protest that successfully ejected a once-feared Syrian military occupation that for decades had smothered their country. At the same time, deadly riots had also broken out across the region in response to cartoons published in Danish newspapers, further consolidating the perception of the region's youth as a horde of intolerant barbarians.

The promise and peril of this time period—amplified by the miracle of the Internet and the rise of social media—fuels the intensity of the anthology's essays. Writers challenged to explore the impact of repression on their daily lives reveal a complex mix of pain and daring imagination. In the societies around them they see daily indignities (a woman in Sudan arrested for wearing pants) and swells of democratic dissent (the massive street protests that broke out in Iran following a rigged 2009 election). And they watch as their outspoken peers push the envelope online via blog posts, Tweets, and viral videos—often paying the price with jail time or worse. In fact, one contest entrant, Kareem Amer, paid dearly for daring to challenge religious and political idols. He was jailed for four years shortly after entering the contest. His crime: a blog post that insulted Egypt's then-president Hosni Mubarak.

Five years later, though, Mubarak is gone while Kareem freely walks the streets of Cairo. The passions coursing through the essays would indeed burst forth in a shockingly powerful way, toppling dictatorships entrenched for decades. Appropriately, the spark that lit the fuse of the entire region was a small indignity. Mohammad Bouazizi, an unemployed Tunisian university graduate turned fruit vendor set himself on fire after being slapped by a policewoman on the streets of Sidi Bouzid, an economically depressed city 150 miles south of the capital, Tunis. Tiny and ostensibly serene Tunisia was suddenly swept by a wave of grassroots protests, and, despite the regime's murderous crackdown and feckless attempts to win back hearts and minds, president-for-life Zine Abidine Ben Ali soon fled. Within days, the dictators in Egypt, Libya, Yemen, Syria, Bahrain, Iran, and beyond would feel the heat of the explosion. (A joke circulated that every dead Arab dictator arriving at the gates of hell had to check one of three boxes to explain his cause of death: coup d'état, Facebook, or Bouazizi.)

RECRUITING DISSIDENT VOICES

One such thinker, albeit from a previous generation, was the Syrian dissident Ammar Abdulhamid, the son of one of Syria's most famous actresses. Abdulhamid had attended university in the United States and become radicalized on campus. But Ayatollah Khomeini's fatwa calling for the death of novelist Salman Rushdie shocked Abdulhamid out of his Islamist phase—an atypical evolution in a region buffeted by Islamism during the last three decades. He returned to Damascus determined to help develop secular civil society and launched an independent publishing house.

In 2005, Abdulhamid had just run afoul of Syria's feared intelligence service and been forced back into exile in the United States. He joined hands with the American Islamic Congress (AIC), a civil rights organization advancing tolerance and the exchange of ideas among Muslims and between other peoples. At the time, the organization was launching its Hands Across the Middle East (HAMSA) initiative to empower the region's youth. The program would subsequently become a major player in the civil rights struggle by training, networking, and advocating for young reformers. One afternoon, Abdulhamid was sitting with staffers from the American Islamic Congress. "The problem is that a vast network of religious extremists offers lots of incentives for young Middle Easterners to radicalize," Abdulhamid mused. "But almost no one is offering incentives for young people to express liberal ideas. What we need is an essay contest on liberty with significant cash prizes!"

This was the anthology's genesis: a flash of genius in the mind of a veteran dissident; the Internet's unfettered horizons; and the determined drive of a few young Americans and Middle Easterners. During the following six years, this vision has paid off handsomely. With Abdulhamid's spark, the "Dream Deferred Essay Contest on Civil Rights in the Middle East" was born. (The contest's name alluded to the African-American writer Langston Hughes's iconic civil rights–era poem.) Private foundations, in particular the Earhart Foundation, responded kindly to a grant proposal for the contest, and enough funds were raised to offer $10,000 annually in prizes for top essays. The Liberty Fund, a nonprofit education resource that publishes elegant editions of books by seminal liberal thinkers, also donated fifty book prizes for honorable mention essays.

To further attract the interest of would-be writers, a cohort of celebrity judges was recruited to help select winners. Entrants thus knew that their essay had the chance to be read by a celebrity or someone they respected. Over the course of the essay contest, a few dozen prominent Americans and Middle Easterners have donated their time to review essays. The inaugural run of the contest attracted luminaries like feminist icon Gloria Steinem; Azar Nafisi, author of the bestseller *Reading Lolita in Tehran;* famed Egyptian civil rights activist Saad Eddin Ibrahim of the Cairo-based Ibn Khaldoun Human Rights Center; and the taboo-busting Moroccan journalist Ahmed Benchemsi, founder of Morocco's hardest hitting publications, *Nichane* and *TelQuel.*

The contest—a twenty-first-century electronic agora—was administered entirely online. A multilingual website taking entries in Arabic, Persian, English, and French asked entrants to answer one of three questions in an essay. To hear the voices of the next generation of civil rights reformers, entrants were required to be under the age of twenty-six. Given the repressive context of their societies and to further encourage them to unlock the secrets of their lives, entrants were given the option to remain anonymous.

The three questions varied slightly from year to year but each was designed to address a particular aspect of the struggle for individual rights. The first question asked writers to share the pain of repression. The second question asked entrants to describe a concrete project that could help strengthen civil rights. And the third question asked thinkers to dream of a better future. Below is a sample of the questions entrants could choose:

1. Identify a civil rights abuse in your local community—how does this repression impact you or someone you know?
2. What would you do with $1,000 to organize a civil rights event or campaign?
3. What is your "dream deferred": a vision of your society with civil rights for all?

The questions were broad but prompted entrants to provide vivid details to buttress lofty ideas. In a deliberate and strategic departure from the usual approach by outsiders to the region's problems, the contest guidelines specifically urged writers not to focus on regional geopolitics or US government policy. Instead, the guidelines explained, "judges are looking for essays that explore what ordinary citizens can do on the grassroots level to strengthen individual rights within Middle Eastern societies." Aside from these prompts, young Middle Easterners were encouraged to be creative in their entries.

When the contest first launched, it was not clear what the response would be. In five years, over eight thousand essays poured in from entrants in twenty-two countries in all four languages. (In this sense, the essay contest was also an excellent activist recruiting tool, as outstanding essayists identified across the Middle East were subsequently invited to AIC-organized regional training workshops and integrated into its grassroots civil rights campaigns.) Some essays, of course, were terrible; many were unremarkable. But out of the mass of entries, dozens stood out, delighting the celebrity judges who reviewed them. This anthology offers a representative sample of those most compelling voices—the results of the essay contest's experiment—to a broad audience.

The framing of the questions around three ideas—pain, action, dreaming—unsurprisingly yielded a potent cocktail of emotional tones in the outstanding essays. Many essayists are shaped by generational frustrations, and some seethe with anger, both rational and irrational. For others, political repression has led to psychological repression. The essayists' identities—whether cultural, ideological, religious, or sexual—are often divided against themselves, forcing more than a few to literally live double lives. But even as they grapple with internal identity clashes, these dissident thinkers are determined to move beyond the rotten paradigms that defined their parents' political lives: pan-Arabism, pan-Islamism, armed struggle, and chauvinistic nationalism.

As befits a contest inspired by an African-American poet, quite a few of the entrants are openly conversant with the Western literary canon and draw inspiration from American civil rights leaders. In a decisive repudiation of cultural relativist dogma, the essayists—including those unfamiliar with liberal thought—reject the notion that individual rights and gender equity are inherently Western concepts or fundamentally incompatible with Middle Eastern religious traditions and cultural mores. Indeed, their voices stand as elegant testaments to the universality of these values. That said, only a few writers embrace coherent, all-encompassing political programs. The emphasis, rather, is on subjective experiences—both tangible and intangible—that engender a set of powerful emotions directed against illegitimate power and irrational authority.

The essay contest itself would have been impossible to run without high levels of Internet penetration in these societies, itself a new phenomenon that shaped the emerging generation targeted by the contest. In a region where for decades all publishing was controlled by regimes and there was no outlet to reach the larger world with personal ideas and human connections, the recent explosion in information technology has opened up Mideast societies as never before. Many essayists turn to the blogosphere to express themselves, often anonymously. Similarly, social media networks such as Facebook, YouTube, and Twitter have allowed Middle Easterners to witness civil rights struggles in neighboring countries and plug into the global community as never before. While ideological, ethnic, and sectarian barriers once divided previous generations, the essays are part of an international dialogue—enabled by the Internet—building a new common civil rights language. After all, the sight of vigilante militias beating activists in Tehran does not look that different from police forces doing the same thing in Tunis.

Despite the impact of the Internet, most essays feature gritty real-world backdrops, which seem integral to the formation of political attitudes and aspirations. The drama of many essays occurs in everyday settings, which become by turn menacing and absurd. It is more often than not in these spaces (hardly ever explored by world media) that our essayists experience the daily humiliations and small victories that define young life in a repressive society. College campus plazas, family dining rooms, public parks, and other seemingly banal places constitute the classrooms where these dissidents obtain their political educations.

By paying close attention to the interplay of these factors, the reader can walk away with a complex psychological profile of the young Mideast dissident—one akin to a diamond with myriad, sometimes contradictory, refractions. The lights beaming forth from these refractions illuminate the origins of today's explosions—and anticipate their future.

FRAMING THE CONVERSATION

Hailing from opposite ends of the region, the coeditors of the anthology embody the dizzying cultural and linguistic diversity of the Middle East. One of us is a Mauritanian Arab (with African and Amazigh roots mixed in); the other is an Iranian (with Azeri roots). Between us, we are fluent in four of the region's languages (Arabic, Persian, French, and Hebrew). While one is primarily a veteran activist and the other a law student and rising intellectual, we have more in common than might first meet the eye. Both of us have fled dictatorial regimes in search of free lives in the West. Precisely because we repeatedly experienced in our personal lives the harsh reality of Mideast repression, we are fiercely committed to liberal democracy. We bring these backgrounds and biases—and psyches scarred by brushes with tyranny—to editing the anthology. This is both our own catharsis and our communion with those left behind under the rule of the world's most entrenched dictators.

Reviewing dozens of winning essays over the years, we were struck by the way many were in dialogue with each other—almost as if these youth were part of a civil rights collective consciousness that remained intangible to most of the world until Iranians took to the streets on a hot summer day in June 2009. To draw out these remarkable connections—linking essayists from vastly different backgrounds—we have organized the essays in the anthology thematically rather than chronologically. The anthology's thematic development mirrors the essay contest questions that inspired the essays: beginning with the pain of repression and slowly building toward civil rights triumphs, both real and imagined.

The anthology opens with essayists who feel "Trapped" and document their frustrations with living under corrupt dictatorships and societal norms that deny individual rights. A wide range of the region's ills is covered, including the silencing of dissent, discrimination against ethno-sectarian and sexual minorities, and gender inequity. While in many instances essayists complain of dictatorial governments, repressive social mores also trap our protagonists. What links these disparate forms of repression, however, is the denial of individual identity by dint of membership in a scorned or subordinate group—be it the sexual identity of a stigmatized Moroccan gay man or the faith of a young Baha'i woman denied access to higher education by Iranian theocrats.

Several essayists—female and male—focus on the obstacles that Middle Eastern women face, and their stories are collected under the section "Unequal." Women's rights came up frequently in essays, and the status of women is a key barometer of the openness of a society. Each essay in this section views the precarious state of women's rights in the region through a different prism. Many shed light on how lack of access to educational and economic opportunities reinforces the fabric of patriarchy. Others discuss sensitive issues, such as so-called honor killings and women's sexuality. Still others decry how travel restrictions and laws targeting immigrants prevent women from fulfilling their full potential.

The anthology concludes on an upbeat note, spotlighting essayists who have "Broken Through" and tell stories of individuals finding the courage to speak out for pluralism, gender equity, and government accountability. These essays describe successful civil rights campaigns and optimistic dreams for a more free future. Some of these breakthroughs are tangible victories (a corrupt teacher held to account here, a bullying writer's union boss forced to back down there). Others recount "spiritual" breakthroughs that lead essayists to come to terms with the power of their own convictions. Other essayists break through simply by imagining, in concrete detail, the changes they would like to see in their societies. While the grand visions of social and political transformation offered by these writers may have sounded implausible when their essays were first submitted, they seem remarkably prescient in light of the democratic bursts rocking the Mideast today.

While the essays in the anthology span a wide range of countries and civil rights challenges, they in no way offer a definitive take on the Middle East. Discussions of geopolitics, for one, are largely absent from the book, as was the case with the essay contest. While intense international tensions are part of the underlying reality from which these voices spring, the essay contest (as noted above) focused on the impact of civil rights repression on the individual lives of young Middle Easterners. Recognizing that so much of the conversation about the Mideast is already framed in geopolitical terms, we were happy to eschew geopolitics in favor of subjective, personal insights that provide Western audiences a fresh perspective on the region.

Likewise, there are no essays bearing directly on the Israeli-Palestinian conflict. This reflects neither the desire to write out Israelis nor indifference to the plight of both peoples. Their conflict, though, has for decades consumed Western attention, with billions of dollars, trillions of words, and endless diplomatic and civic initiatives thrown at it. While often referred to as *the* "Middle East Conflict," the reduction of a large and diverse region to what happens on a tiny sliver of land led many to be surprised by the Iranian uprising of 2009 and the 2011 Arab revolts. Putting an end to the tragic collision of nationalisms in the Levant will not resolve the deeper internal conflicts between citizens and rulers in the Mideast. The creation of a Palestinian state, while of historic importance, will not gain Saudi women the right to drive or help young Iranians surmount Internet censorship. A state there, or a treaty here, are of little incidence to the Middle East's struggle for civil rights, which transcends the region's geopolitical conflicts.

In choosing essays for the anthology, we did not practice "affirmative action." The selection process was entirely merit based, with only the most compelling pieces included. Certain civil rights challenges roiling the region are thus not directly addressed, for example, sectarian repression in Bahrain and Oman and labor abuses in the United Arab Emirates. Budgetary constraints also limited essay contest entries to four languages, and the linguistic scope of the anthology is thus more limited than we would have preferred.

Some of the essayists' politics might make readers uneasy. A very few, for example, seem to implicitly support the establishment of Islamic governance in their countries—even as they unequivocally condemn political violence committed in the name of Islam. The anthology in no way endorses the specific agendas put forth by every contributor. But we felt it was important not to sugarcoat the region's realities. Western audiences should encounter these voices and consider the promise—and limitations—of reform movements not always populated by perfect Jeffersonian democrats.

Other readers, meanwhile, might be made uncomfortable or even shocked by essays that boldly tread on taboo territories. So be it. Essayists addressing topics like homosexuality and female virginity in Muslim-majority countries deserve to be heard. These topics were not specifically elicited by the contest, and it was initially surprising that so many essayists chose to reveal—in intimate, sometimes painful, detail—the price they have paid for expressing their sexual identities. Their courage compelled us not to primp up reality so as to avoid offending certain sensibilities. If anything, we felt a moral responsibility to amplify Mideast voices too often suffocated for defying traditional norms.

It also bears noting that the vast majority of the essayists represented in the anthology are not professional journalists or writers. While a small number of the contributors are remarkably lucid English prose stylists, most submitted their pieces in Arabic or Persian. After carefully translating them, we rigorously edited the essays for clarity—without altering their underlying substance. In a handful of cases, we deliberately brought to the foreground dramatic elements already embedded in the essays themselves. Where absolutely necessary, we have provided footnotes clarifying references and allusions that might otherwise be unfamiliar to Western readers. Each essay is also framed by an introductory editors' note explaining the socio-historical context in which it was written and, where available, offering biographical details about the author. Additionally, interspersed throughout the anthology are profiles of and interviews with some of the essayists and contest judges. These interviews were conducted at various points over the preceding years, often in conjunction with the announcement of each year's winning essays.

Finally, a note about the anthology's title. Work on compiling and editing these essays began well before grassroots protests exploded across North Africa in early 2011. The project's working title was "Re-Orient," an allusion to Edward Said's landmark 1978 text *Orientalism,* which critiqued Western traditions of exoticizing the Middle East. We saw the anthology as extending Said's thesis—sometimes in subversive ways—by challenging

American audiences to see beyond the geopolitical headlines to the grass-roots civil rights struggle bubbling largely unnoticed below the surface. Hence, Re-Orient.

Then, within the span of weeks, the entire region suddenly "got Tunisified"—as one running Twitter meme aptly described the sequential explosion of pro-democracy revolts. In the West, that sequence has come to be known by the moniker "Arab Spring"—a phrase that is in many ways problematic. First, it risks essentializing the highly diverse Middle East as "Arab," when the region comprises all sorts of ethnic and sectarian groups. Indeed, Iran has only a small (and repressed) Arab minority. Second, the bubbly term "spring" evoked the giddy headlines of Marxist magazines from decades ago that would hail the arrival of a national "spring" every time socialists won elections in a particular corner of the planet. Spring was also a somewhat inappropriate seasonal metaphor for describing a process that, at least in the northern hemisphere, began in the dead of winter.

Nevertheless, the anthology's ultimate title directly evokes the notion of an "Arab Spring" so as to situate the essayists at the center of the unfolding Western conversation about the historic transformations unfolding in the Middle East. The intent is by no means to glibly regurgitate the naïve optimism and euphoric politics that have come to orbit this term but rather to soberly scrutinize it. Not only does the anthology undermine a simplistic view of the region as "Arab," but its content and editorial framing suggest that what lies at the end of the Arab Spring rainbow may not necessarily be the sorts of liberal societies the essayists aspire to.

But we shall leave these debates for a later time. For now, enjoy this special opportunity to listen in as some of the region's fascinating young dissidents share their experiences, frustrations, and aspirations. Set aside any preconceived notions about the Middle East, and engage these essayists on their own terms. Who knows, maybe you will even be inspired to respond to their rallying cries.

PART I

TRAPPED

"The fear that flows in my blood like fish eggs in deep seawater, how can I dodge it?"

—Muhammad al-Maghut

"I AM NOT AYMAN!"

Anonymous—Egypt—Age 22

Egypt, the most populous Arab nation, was for a good part of the twentieth century the Arab Middle East's political and cultural engine. During the first half of the century, the country boasted a relatively pluralistic society ruled by a weak monarchy not entirely free from British meddling—despite the country's formal independence in 1922. Attracted by a dynamic economy as embodied by Cairo's stock market—one of the region's first—European expats were drawn to pre-Nasser Egypt. Religious minorities like Egyptian Jews and Christian Copts also thrived.

This relatively prosperous period, however, was marred by entrenched poverty among Egyptian peasants, as well as by the monarchy's inability to rid itself of corruption. Not long after independence, the Muslim Brotherhood was born as a reaction to the wide secularist influence on the country's affairs. Despite being formally banned for much of their history, the "Brothers" have exerted enormous influence on Egyptian society and the wider Muslim Mideast—and continue to do so today.

Modern Egypt is more closely associated with the brand of Arab nationalism embodied by Colonel Gamal Abdel Nasser. Leading a "Free Officers' Movement," Nasser seized control of the country in a bloodless coup in July 1952, unseating Egypt's last monarch, King Farouk. Nasser and his heirs violently suppressed the Brotherhood and instituted military rule that persists to this day—despite the nonviolent 2011 revolution that overthrew longstanding dictator General Muhammad Hosni Mubarak. While nominally secularist, the Mubarak regime—like those preceding it—was deeply *illiberal. This regime suffocated Egyptian civil society while, in a perverse dynamic, empowered reactionary voices like the Brotherhood.*

In our opening essay, the contributor places herself in the shoes of a closeted Egyptian gay man and describes his frustrated attempts to stay true to his identity against enormous pressure exerted by a repressive state and an intolerant society. The essay was written against the backdrop of the so-called Queen Boat Incident in 2001, when Egyptian police raided a floating disco on the Nile, arresting fifty-two men who were without female partners. The suspects were subjected to invasive physical examinations to "establish" their homosexuality, accused of being "agents of Israel," and tried on a range of vice charges.

The incident received a great deal of attention from both the regional and Western media. The Egyptian government's sudden crackdown on a tolerated underground gay scene—vividly described by our essayist—was shocking and unexpected to Egyptians and outside observers alike. It crystalized the precarious nature of individual liberty in Mideast societies, where civil rights restrictions are not always enforced but can suddenly spring into effect at the whim of rulers.

The protagonist's inability to translate his web-based identity into the real world parallels the essayist's own self-censorship. For while she offered what is most likely a fictionalized account, the contributor nevertheless insisted that her piece be published anonymously.

THE SCREECH OF TIRES SNAPPED HIM BACK TO ATTENTION, RE-placing the thoughts buzzing around his brain with an anxious immediacy. He stared at the cab driver behind the wheel, her mouth opening and closing over and over for no apparent reason. Her fillings flashed silver at him every few seconds. Her windows were up, rendering her comically mute despite her traffic-induced rage. He had had enough. He would walk the rest of the way. As he did, his mental disarray did not prevent him from giving due respect to the nonexistence of traffic laws in Cairo.

He approached the alleyway that served as one of the city's pickup spots, noting with equal amounts of jealousy and fear the men standing around.

They swaggered, clothes torn and tight in the style associated with male homosexuality. Their faces attempted rebellious outrage with courage implied in their plucked eyebrows and slightly rouged cheeks, these visible signs distinguishing them from "real men." And yet he imagined he could detect in them an uncertainty—trepidation born from knowing that others had been taken away for doing just this on other Mondays, Wednesdays, Anydays. He imagined he could see in their cocky stances a readiness for flight.

He had picked this particular spot knowing that it was slightly less conspicuous than others, just in case it were to turn out that he had been tricked all along, and that he had cultivated a relationship with a decoy. He saw Tariq standing a few meters away, wearing the blue striped shirt he had been told to look out for. Never in their online conversations had he shared with Tariq a picture of himself, preferring safe anonymity to the promise of future intimacy. He had not worn his blue-striped shirt, telling himself he did not like the way it looked on him. He could do enough recognizing for both of them.

He held back, trying not to stare at the man he had been talking to for the past eight months. They had planned numerous meetings before. He had many times approached the date with queasy anticipation, calling it off at the last minute. A fictitious business trip one time, an imagined death in the family another. Tariq's patience had brought him here today. A vice informant would not wait this long, he told himself. An informant would not invest so much time creating plausible details.

Or would he? He looked around once more, suspicious, trying to find ill will lurking in the faces subjected to his exacting scrutiny. He cleared his throat. Then he took what he imagined some novelists he had read meant by "a measured breath." Sweat trickled into his eyes, a burning rivulet of building anxiety he was trying to keep under control. He turned toward Tariq, preparing for a step, only to be rooted to the spot when their eyes met. Tariq smiled tentatively, hesitated, and then started forward, perhaps deciding that the physical description traded online so many times matched enough to counter the absence of blue stripes.

He felt panic rising in him. His eyes searched frantically in Tariq's clothing for telltale signs of hidden handcuffs, a gun, something, anything out of the ordinary. He debated what to do, realizing that he was out of time when Tariq stopped in front of him, smiling shyly. "Ayman?" He had forgotten for a moment that he had never given his real name (yet another safety measure). He looked around frantically, switching his gaze from one potentially menacing figure to the next in the gloomy dark. He was suddenly screaming, his lungs expelling the night's mistrust in hot, hysterical denial:

"I am not Ayman! I am not Ayman! Get away from me, you faggot!"

He turned around, not noticing everyone around him likewise fleeing, the disturbance upsetting a confidence made fragile by stories of baton rapes, capture, jail, and ruined lives. Like a flock of nervous gazelles prepared by natural selection for a life of constant victimization, they ran. He eventually flagged down a cab. His ragged breath and frenzied thoughts slowed down to normalcy. He got home, turned on his computer, and started an email:

"Tariq *habibi*—sorry I couldn't make it." He paused, searching. Would Tariq believe that the person he met earlier tonight was someone else? He decided, just in case, to erect one more barricade against identification. "One of my patients needed an emergency C-section. Maybe we can try this again soon? Yours, Ayman." An ob-gyn, he mused. He would read up on the field tomorrow, to be able to speak authoritatively about it the next time they chatted online.

He turned his computer off, realizing for the first time how tired he was. He sat hunched over for a while, thinking about the events of the night. He looked around his apartment—a testament to how diligently he had disguised his "criminality" from everyone around him out of fear of imprisonment or worse. His apartment, he thought, was very masculine. He bought furniture only in muted, dark colors, fearing his neighbors (all potential informers) might find his tastes too flamboyant for a man. Expensively framed prints of female nudes decked his walls, replacing the *Playboy* and Haifa Wahbi* posters of his college days.

---

* Lebanese model, actress, and singer.

His daytime persona, too, was carefully designed to project straightness. He had cultivated a gruff rumble of a voice, so different from the soft-spoken stereotype Egypt had of its gay men. He went to the gym religiously, a result of once having been called a sissy by a drunk in the street. He looked over at his computer, the only vehicle through which his sexuality could find expression—as long as it remained unclaimed by a name, a picture, an address, or any other carelessly overlooked detail.

He wondered at times whether he overreacted, whether what he had to fear was more in his head than a real threat. He was well aware that his paranoia knew no bounds, and yet he saw it as more of a protective mechanism than an oppressive one. He knew, despite his wonderings and what-ifs, that his secret must never know another. He thought of the recent Queen Boat incident. He reminded himself of the harsh sentences handed down to the young men captured that day, the forced anal exams used to "prove" homosexual conduct, the bogus charges of prostitution and drug possession. He turned off the lights on his nudes, his brown leather couches, his sports magazines, and made his way to the bedroom.

It was the time when he felt least alone, lying in the dark as he was now, imagining all of the men like him dreaming impossible dreams. Sometimes he imagined ridiculous happy endings for all of those sad little lives in their little Cairo flats. He never dared think of one for himself, though, lest his dreams lead to incautious action. He had long ago resigned himself to a life of missed connections and fleeting intimacy. He wondered for a short moment how he would explain his many fabrications to Tariq if and when they met at last. Would that entire cities, countries, governments could change for them! He rolled over, closed his eyes, and turned himself off.

MONOLOGUE WITH THE PRINCE

K.N.—Saudi Arabia—Age 25

Saudi Arabia is named after the family which, during the early twentieth century, forcibly united hitherto autonomous tribes and provinces in the Arabian Peninsula to form a monarchic state. At the time of its founding in 1932, the House of Saud struck a bargain with the ultra-conservative Arab clerical class, giving it free reign over all social matters in exchange for legitimacy.

Modern Saudi Arabia is a welfare state funded by enormous oil and gas revenues. Citizens are exempted from paying taxes and provided with free state-funded education and health care. These privileges—as enticing they may be—are not part of a social contract as understood in the West. They do not give rise to citizenship rights and duties but rather operate as one half of a corrupt trade: the ruling monarchs administer their country's natural resources by divine right and without any checks and balances on their power; citizens receive privileges in exchange for absolute submission to the rulers. Non-governmental and other civil society organizations are banned in the Kingdom, and no citizen is allowed to belong to or form any political group. Free speech is severely curtailed, and individual liberties are not recognized as such.

Lately, against a backdrop of soaring unemployment and a massive youth bulge (in a country suffocated by octogenarian royals), the regime's corruption and mismanagement have increasingly jeopardized even this basic social bargain. Our next essayist paints a vivid portrait of the impact of this breakdown on Saudi youth.

I FELT SO LUCKY WHEN I WAS SELECTED FROM AMONG THOU-
sands of students to be one of six representing my university at the Expedi-
tionary Forum for National Dialogue. The Forum was supposed to tackle
issues of tolerance, development, and—remarkably for Saudi Arabia—free
expression. As its name suggested, the central theme of the Forum was dialogue. I was thrilled to get a chance to express myself in a public setting, if
just this once.

But it was not meant to be. Just before we headed to the Forum, a senior
university official warned us to be very careful about what we said. "Better yet," he admonished us, "don't say anything at all." The Forum is just a
"formality," he explained, so best not get too excited thinking it was going to
change anything in this country.

He was right. Before we were even allowed to enter the conference center,
one of the Forum leaders—a ridiculous figure with a stern face—appeared
before us to set the "ground rules." "I warn you," he yelled. "I warn you to
measure every word before uttering it." Some dialogue.

The sessions themselves consisted of one official after another lecturing
us. The agendas and topics of discussion were all preset and non-negotiable.
The first speaker was the minister of education, Dr. Mohammad al-Rasheed,
pontificating on the finer points of state education policy. I was briefly heartened to see a few students raise their hands after his talk was over. Would they
actually challenge him? Would they question the repressive nature of Saudi
universities?

If only. The "questions" were actually expressions of the most nauseat-
ing flattery prewritten by the Forum organizers. (Still, you had to admire the
students for reading the dull queries as earnestly and diligently as they could.)
The Forum only went downhill from there—one self-important government
deputy minister and policy adviser after another droned on and on at us for
what seemed like an eternity.

The headline session, billed as the most important, hosted His Royal
Highness Abdul-Majeed bin Abdul-Azeez al-Saud, prince of Mecca. A few
minutes before the prince's arrival in a seemingly endless convoy of black
Mercedes sedans, we were ordered to leave the main conference room and

move up to the second-floor balcony area. When we arrived there, we found ourselves surrounded by dozens of security officers, both uniformed and plainclothes, all armed to the teeth. It seemed as though there were more policemen than students! It was hot and claustrophobic on the balcony, while the floor below was almost empty save for a few Forum leaders and journalists.

His Royal Highness gave a speech you could read in the opinion pages of any third world newspaper, repeating the usual clichés: "We have to thank God that our country is one of the best in the world, for the wisdom of our royal family, and for the wise government officials who provide us with security and safety around the clock . . . ." And on and on. (As for reform, he explained that it was coming but that it would call for patience, a *lot* of patience, because change comes slowly. . . .)

While the prince was ranting and raving about the many blessings of Saudi life, I heard the voice of the Egyptian comedian Adil Imam saying his famous comic phrase: "There she goes again!" At first, I thought I was daydreaming—only to find out that the voice was coming from my friend Mansour's cellular phone. He played that clip over and over. My attempts to stop him were in vain. I thought we were all about to get into big trouble. But, hey, that was Mansour's way of "dialoging" with the Prince. He inspired other students, who played the sound of fireworks on their phones. In our culture, this signals that the speaker is lying. Suppressed laughter was heard. The officers started getting suspicious but eventually decided it was just a matter of kids being kids.

A few minutes later, the prince finished his speech and left without addressing questions or comments.

I did not find a way to express myself freely until I started my own blog about a year after the Forum. On my blog, I can share some of my viewpoints and feelings—even though what I publish constitutes less than a fifth of what I actually think. My friends and family members are concerned about my activities in the Arabic blogosphere. They remind me of the many Arab bloggers who are jailed—or worse—for committing political thought crimes on the Internet. Some of those jailed for thinking inappropriate thoughts are kept imprisoned even after finishing their long sentences.

I appreciate my friends' concern, but I do not understand how a human being can live without expressing himself. How long can we endure this suffocating atmosphere? Although we live in a country whose oil incomes rank as highest in the world, prices are soaring, unemployment among the youth is high, and even those who find jobs are barely able to make ends meet.

It is my right to live a dignified life and enjoy the blessings of freedom. Until that moment arrives, I shall continue to share at least some of my thoughts with the world. Hell, the prince sure isn't listening. So let the political police knock on my door and haul me off. As for my friend Mansour, he need not worry about the secret police. Six months after the Forum, we heard that he had martyred himself in Iraq.

LIVING INSIDE 1984

S.D.—Iran—Age 21

Modern Iran was born when, in the early 1920s, Reza Khan, an officer in the Persian Cossack Brigade, overthrew the stale and decrepit Qajar dynasty that had ruled the country for the better part of two centuries. Reza crowned himself emperor and embarked on an aggressive program of modernization and secularization, transforming a backward, illiterate country dominated by two great powers, Britain and Russia, into a modern nation state. In 1941, however, the Allies—concerned by Reza Shah's pro-Axis sympathies and the need to secure Iranian oil fields—forced him to abdicate in favor of his son, Muhammad Reza, often recalled as "the Shah" in the West.

Muhammad Reza took up where his father left off, using Iran's grow-ing oil wealth to develop industry, combat illiteracy, and establish modern institutions. He also instituted aggressive land reforms, empowered women and minorities, and sought to limit the influence of Shi'a clerics. (Unlike most of their Sunni Arab counterparts, the majority of Iranians subscribe to Shi'a Islam. Shi'ism sanctifies the Prophet's direct blood lineage—and most especially one of Muhammad's descendants, Mahdi, known as the "hidden" imam, since he is said to be in a state of divine occultation pending the Apocalypse.)

While the Shah provided Iranians with many social and individual freedoms, he brooked no political dissent. In 1953, with some American and British assistance, he overthrew a populist prime minister who, in seeking to nationalize Iranian oil, challenged his power. Toward the end of his reign, the Shah became increasingly autocratic and erratic. Corrup-tion in his palace angered poor Iranians while also alienating the emerging educated middle class that was no longer willing to accept a 2,500-year old tradition of Persian absolutism. In 1979, he was overthrown by a coalition of Islamists, leftists, and liberals—and led by the stern Ayatollah Khomeini.

While in exile under the Shah, Khomeini preached popular sovereignty, individual liberty, and egalitarianism. Once in power, however, he quickly disposed of his "coalition partners" (via execution) and established the regime that misrules Iran to this day. The Islamic Republic of Iran derives its legitimacy from a Shi'a doctrine—mostly concocted by Khomeini—known as the guardianship of the jurisconsult. Under this theory, absolute power rests in the hands of a small clerical class and, more specifically, a "Supreme Leader," who rules in the absence of Imam Mahdi.

In practice, the guardianship translates into a profoundly undemocratic and illiberal state, where dissidents, women, and ethno-sectarian minorities are repressed and individual rights are virtually nonexistent. While the Islamic Republic constitution provides for a few nominally democratic elements, in reality, these are structurally incapable of advancing liberal reforms since their acts are subject to the Supreme Leader's absolute veto power. The Leader also controls the judiciary, the armed forces, and the media. All of these institutions are engineered to help perpetuate the regime.

Our next essay, from Iran, is one of the most chilling in the anthology, not because it relates a gruesome account of state violence, but because it painstakingly describes what happens to a free mind living under a brutal theocracy like the Islamic Republic. It is also a deeply personal portrait of a young man's realization of the "doublethink" that pervades his society.

CONDITIONS HERE ARE TOO LUDICROUS TO BELIEVE. WHILE YOU are fighting for the rights of pandas over there, people are still being stoned to death here in my country. While your feminists are obsessed with reappropriating the unappreciated works of turn-of-the-century female writers, I still hear mullahs preach on state TV that "women should not watch male athletes compete!" While you are debating the risks associated with children's exposure to violence in video games, our kids watch a convict—who, by the way, has not been afforded any procedural rights—wiggle to his last breath right in front of their eyes. (They may even relish this *cool* experience for a short while, but they will be haunted by nightmares for the rest of their lives.)

Iran, my homeland, is where I was born and raised. And, like millions of others, I was taught to be grateful to God for bestowing on me—undeservedly, of course—the best country to live in, the best faith to follow, and the best rulers to be subject to.

I do not know how it all started to change for me, but I am sure it was not a matter of choice. All I did was learn "some" English and fall in love with literature—something that has been stifled into a coma in my country for many years. Before long, I found myself enjoying *1984, Fahrenheit 451,* and reading over and over Auden's "The Unknown Citizen." Gradually, I became conscious of my deep-rooted hatred of totalitarian regimes. An amusing and disturbing feeling found its way into my heart as I drew parallels between the fictitious societies depicted by the likes of Orwell and Bradbury and what actually happens in my own. (Whenever I saw our beloved Supreme Leader Khamenei's cold eyes staring down at me ominously from public murals, I would pathetically attempt to convince myself that he was *not* Big Brother—that he could not be.)

After a while, the dystopian fictions seemed more saddening than amusing to me, as if they were written solely to tease me. The way I felt was not much different from what Romeo and Juliet's parents would have felt if they had just seen the play. The pain was just too real.

Literature helped me realize the fact that we—Iranian Shi'ite Muslims—are not the only creatures endowed with a brain to think and a heart to feel. It might seem a dull truism to you, but not to one who has been living all his life in an isolated, perennially self-righteous society.

With new eyes I saw new things. The truths turned into big lies, big lies into bitter truths, and miracles faded into commonplace accidents. I became obsessed with paradoxes that could not be reconciled in any way. Not that I had not been aware of them before. Only, I used to trace them back to my own mind rather than to my social reality. "Who the hell am I to defy *his holiness?*" I used to remind myself. But little by little, these faint ideas turned into beliefs, and at the time when I was losing faith in everything, they became my only convictions.

Then came the lies, loads of them, from everywhere. Sometimes they were so gross that I really wondered if they were lies or the fantastical projections of my own mind. How could our president declare that "we are the freest nation in the world" and get away with it? How could he boast that "there are no prisoners of conscience in Iran"—when their dead bodies are daily hauled off from Iran's notorious political prisons?

Eventually I found some answers to these questions. Our leaders are inspired to build towering cities of lies because they are bound and blinded by The Truth. If you believe you are absolutely right, then every terror, every lie, every act of torture, even every murder, loses its ghastliness. The crimes suddenly turn into undesirable but necessary measures to uphold the sacred regime, the lesser evils, so to speak, and all that nonsense.

Of course, our rulers are not the only ones who have resorted to these kinds of methods. Let us be practical. Every group believes in things that it holds to be True, and certainly sometimes, if not always, acts according to the ancient motto that the ends justify the means. But there are moral limits to applying these means, and it is the utter disregard for these limits that makes repressive regimes like Iran's what they are.

And what exactly are these limits? Human rights—but only insofar as they are conceived as being both fundamental and universal. Hence what our rulers say about "Islamic human rights"—their feckless attempts to frame rights "according to our historical traditions and religious mores"—is just another one of their big lies. Unfortunately, too many Iranians have bought into the clerics' sophistry. What your children know by heart—what is natural and "self-evident" to them—is alien to many of my adult compatriots. The blame for this sad state of affairs belongs to, among others, our grotesque state-run media, which do their best to distort the facts and provide a schizophrenic image of the outside world.

The apocalyptic messianism of the Shi'a—their relentless zeal for purifying the "corrupted world"—doesn't help either. Islam is the central driving force in many Middle Eastern lives. Yet what makes Iran's case so special is the way the state makes use of this binding force to manipulate its subjects. The Islamic Republic of Iran claims to have found the perfect middle ground between Islam and democracy. Perhaps—if we do not want to be obsessed with conspiracy theories—this was our founders' "original intent." But what has been realized since then is far from it. There has never been a middle ground. (When they had the reins of power during the 1990s, the reformists attempted to lay the foundations for democracy on the enormous, misty sphere of Islam. They failed.)

The Islamic Republic's legitimacy is based wholly on a peculiar interpretation of Islam justifying absolutism and dictatorship. The regime expends enormous amounts of energy institutionalizing this version of the faith. This is why political rhetoric and religious dogma are so intermingled in Iran. It is also why the most ardent supporters of the state are, according to the regime's ideologues, the most pious among us. But I suspect that if suddenly and without the due preparation, the current system of government were to collapse, many Iranians would, as the saying goes, "lose their faith" and form the biggest community of atheists on the planet.

The web and social media have made significant inroads toward breaking the regime's grip on the public mind, and particularly on youthful minds. Even so, our fears outweigh our hopes. There is a long and difficult road ahead, and the light at the end of the tunnel is ever so dim. In the meantime, I imagine I will be spending a lot of time with my dear friend Orwell.

WANTED FOR DREAMING: S.D. STAYS UNDERGROUND

When "S.D." entered the essay contest, he had to balance what he calls the "insatiable need to share my misery with the world" against the fear of being exposed and arrested if he won. Interviewed in 2008 from an undisclosed location (for security reasons) in his native Iran, the contest winner explained how he is handling both the excitement and the danger.

Are you afraid now that you won the contest?

I'd be lying if I said no. I'm worried—that's why I don't want my real name publicized. Even before I decided to write the essay, I knew there was the risk of being exposed if I won. Still, my essay is in English, and the essay contest was not exactly advertised on public billboards in Iran. It's not my friends but rather my parents that I'm worried about. I don't want to hurt their feelings or fail to be their prodigal son.

Your essay suggests that Iran's older generation has failed—will your generation be different?

Of course we will be different, but it is hard to gauge how different we will be from our fathers. The ideology that the state nourishes can't last long. People of my generation feel something has to change. Sparkles of change are flashing in our minds, especially in the minds of those who can connect to the Internet and get facts. The Internet has revolutionized everything—for instance, that's how I learned about the essay contest.

How did you come to think critically about repression in your society?

There was not one moment. But I do remember when I was seven, taking a tour of Khomeini's residence in northern Tehran. We were a bunch of kids staring at a little room through glass doors at a pair of his slippers and a white sheet-covered couch. All my friends started sniffling and crying. I tried to squeeze my eyes against the panes and ooze out some tears. But I could not. Then we were taken to the mosque next to the house where Khomeini used to give speeches. Everyone resumed their crying, yet I could not. There were sharp pangs of guilt gnawing at my conscience. I stole glances at my peers crying at something I couldn't summon tears for. See how deeply these bonds have been implanted in our subconscious! Now imagine that these kids have to grow up and realize their "Revered Leader" might have made some serious mistakes; that they have to trust their own individuality and seek their basic rights. This is a painful odyssey we have to go through alone as we crawl our way, all by ourselves, out of the dark tunnels of fanaticism to the light of doubt.

LEAVING AHLAM BEHIND

B. al-Mutairi—Kuwait—Age 25

*"Speaker al-Khurafi orders guards to drive audience out;
guards unable due to hall enthusiasm . . . Speaker adjourns
legislative session for half hour, demanding hall cleared."*

—*Al-Qabas*, May 16, 2006

*"Al-Khurafi says he was not inclined to use force to drive the
audience out, because 'these are, at the end, our own sons and
daughters.'"*

—*Al-Watan*, May 16, 2006

*Kuwait is best remembered in the West for its harrowing ordeal after Iraqi
dictator Saddam Hussein invaded and laid it waste over an unsettled debt
in 1990. The tiny oil-rich country has been ruled since the 1750s by the
al-Sabah dynasty whose origins lay in Saudi Arabia's Najd Province. In
its heyday, the al-Sabah dynasty gave refuge to the man who would later
found modern-day Saudi Arabia—the future King Abdulaziz al-Saud. As
such, the dynasty was an important power broker in the region during the
pre-oil era.*

*At the dawn of the colonial period, the al-Sabah entered into an alliance with the British, consolidated later when the first oil discoveries were
made, affording Kuwaitis the protection and independence they sought from
their larger, more powerful neighbors: Iraq, Saudi Arabia, and, across the*

Persian Gulf, Iran. Upon gaining its independence from Britain in 1961, the sleepy sheikhdom was reborn as the modern State of Kuwait.

Kuwait, with its 3.6 million inhabitants, is a paradox. The country's glitzy façade of material wealth and modernity stands in stark contrast to many of the region's countries. Kuwait boasts an active parliamentary opposition and a loud press—the envy of other liberal Gulf reformers. Women fought for and obtained universal suffrage in 2005. Even more interesting, Kuwaiti society is considerably less socially conservative than, say, either Saudi Arabia or Iran.

But Kuwait is no model of civil rights. The country has Roman-style citizenship laws, and five categories of citizenship, restricting many of its people's basic rights. Another group, the "bidoon" (lit. without), descendants of nomadic tribes originating from Iraq and Saudi Arabia, lack citizenship rights altogether. Since the contract of citizenship in Kuwait—as in other Gulf states—is one where citizens trade submission for access to state welfare, Kuwaiti elites view naturalization of the bidoon as a direct threat to their own incomes. The same treatment also applies to the legions of expatriates living in Kuwait, who are hardly ever granted citizenship and, even when they are, cannot run for parliament or high office.

Our next essayist and her friends set out to change this state of affairs from within the system but then must watch as a regime structurally resistant to change stifles their potential and suffocates their activist spirit.

THE HEADLINES AND NEWS STORIES—WRITTEN FROM THE PERspective of the powerful—did not capture our anguish that day. But I still remember how my friend Ahlam was crying bitterly over my shoulder after we were driven out of the National Assembly, accused of "rioting" when all we had done was stage a peaceful protest against government corruption. Ahlam could not take the humiliation. Me, I was left numb. Much of what I remember of that day is in the form of a disjointed collage of painful images and emotions.

Ahlam wanted to scream and shout. But screaming is not a civilized form of expression. So she desperately sought out journalists from *al-Qabas* and *al-Watan* who might tell our side of the story. She was quickly disappointed. The journalists were no freer than she was—constrained as they were by numerous invisible red lines and unwritten laws. (Things have only gotten worse since then as the government has raised another Damoclean sword over the heads of Kuwaiti journalists, who now face the prospect of imprisonment, in addition to the usual work bans, for crossing certain lines.)

It all started when we heard about rampant corruption among members of the Kuwaiti parliament, usually treated as beyond reproach by the subservient press. The people themselves discuss such matters in hushed tones. But they know full well who really runs the show. Seeking a government job? Then you'd better have the backing of a magnanimous MP. In need of urgent medical treatment abroad? Then you must resort to the "right" MP and hope he woke up on the right side of his bed that morning. Received a failing grade as a college student? Then you'd best make it clear that you voted for—you guessed it—the right MP.

The parliamentarians' "magic touch" is needed to grease the wheels and solve all problems, big and small—problems they themselves have been creating for many years by promoting patronage and dependency instead of efficiency and transparency. After all, if the country and its people really started to move forward, what would Kuwaiti politicians shed their crocodile tears over? What would they scream about to prove their heroism and sensitivity to the needs of the "dispossessed"?

After years of frustration, my activist friends and I decided that to deal with corruption in Kuwaiti politics, a gradualist approach is the best way forward. The first step would be to broaden and diversify each MP's constituency. If each legislator had to serve Sunni *and* Shi'a citizens, city-dwellers *and* bedouins, he would be more likely to prioritize the needs of the country as a whole over his own narrow, tribal interests. This way, we would slowly break the grip of corruption on the National Assembly.

That was the hope anyway. But as soon as we launched our campaign, we were accused of being puppets of external forces and special interest groups. Even worse, we were derided as being spoiled, privileged little brats with nothing better to do than stick our noses where they do not belong. (Never mind that youth constitute 65 percent of Kuwait's population.) We were undeterred, eventually taking our message all the way to the National Assembly—only to be forcibly driven out and ridiculed in the press.

The problem, of course, goes beyond "machine politics" lording it over Kuwait City. At the heart of the country's inability to move forward is the state's disdain for freedom of expression and genuine politics. Sadly, the disdain for freedom is often only reinforced by the culture at large.

Take, for example, the right to vote. During the last electoral cycle, Kuwaiti women were finally granted suffrage. Admittedly, this was a huge step forward for the country. But despite winning suffrage, Kuwaiti women like me were still unable to exercise meaningful political choice. As voting day approached, my brother started badgering me to vote for his favorite candidate. It did not matter what the man's qualifications and policy positions were. All that mattered was his tribal background and the fact that he shared our last name. To my annoyance, my beloved uncle did the very same thing. To the men in our family, my vote mattered only to the extent that it would advance our tribal interests. Otherwise, I was altogether excluded from political conversations around the dinner table. It was understood that—despite having the right to vote—I had nothing to add to the debate. And this tragic situation was not just limited to my family or tribe. The education system and the media have, by and large, failed to bring women into the national conversation.

Because no politician attempted to persuade me—as a Kuwaiti woman—to vote for him "on the merits," so to speak, I decided to cast a protest vote. Out of spite, I cast a clear, blank vote. (I believe in cleanliness because it is next to godliness!)

Freedom of expression, too, is something to be feared in Kuwait. If a voice falls in the minority on a particular issue, it is not enough to we debate that voice on the substance of the matter; we must exclude it altogether. This is why, I suspect, my mother often sneaks into my room to tear up political articles and notes, fearing that they might criticize an MP or other politician whose favors our family may need one day. When I protest, she gets furious. "You are being fed the best food, you wear the nicest clothes, what else do you have to complain about?" she screams. I tell her that I am only seeking to put my God-given mind to good use, not to "undermine national security." But to no avail.

I am not the only one in this position. Many of my activist friends and fellow thinkers are in the same boat. Since the disastrous protest we staged at the National Assembly, many of the young women involved have been silenced out of fear. Others have been married off. They avoid politics altogether, knowing their husbands disapprove of their activism. (The word "politics" in Arabic, by the way, is a feminine noun.) Still others have been discouraged by the slow pace of change. Some interned for non-governmental organizations, only to realize that the NGO leaders, fond of projecting the image of "intellectuals," are just as parochial and narrow-minded as the rest of society. They operate according to the same prehistoric mindsets as our parents, teachers, and parliamentarians.

As I write, I am preparing to go abroad to explore the world outside and study for a while. I am saddened to leave behind my only friend still committed to effecting change in Kuwait—despite the many political and cultural obstacles she faces.

Her name, Ahlam, means "dreams" in Arabic.

SEEKING SALVATION

M.M.—Algeria—Age 23

In 1962, Algeria threw off the yoke of 130 years of French colonialism. Prior to its independence, Algeria's status within the French empire was not one of a "colony" but rather an integral part of France extended into North Africa. Yet France's ideals of "liberty, equality, and fraternity" were not extended to Algeria's Muslims, who were denied full French citizenship. Instead, hundreds of thousands of European settlers were imported, including many Italians, Spaniards, and Portuguese, most of whom fled in 1962 to France after a particularly bloody national liberation struggle.

The colonial period caused lasting damage to the country's cultural fabric and national identity. Algeria is a multi-cultural and multi-ethnic society comprising many groups, most prominently Arabs, Kabyles, Chaouiya Amazighs, and Touaregs. Shortly after kicking out the French, however, Algeria's first president, Ahmed Ben Bella gave a rousing speech (ironically delivered in French), where he declared: "Nous sommes Arabes, nous sommes Arabes!" ("We are Arabs, we are Arabs!"). Such an essentializing declaration did not bode well for the nascent state's ethnic cohesion or political culture. Not surprisingly, Ben Bella was himself deposed in a military coup a few years later in the wake of internal rebellions.

The new strongman who emerged was a battle-hardened commander of the national liberation forces, Colonel Houari Boumediene. Initially a shy man averse to public appearances, he grew into his position and became a classic authoritarian ruler with a cult of personality. Boumediene embarked on large schemes of statist transformation, including government-imposed agrarian reform and massive industrial projects, all funded by Al-

geria's newly discovered oil and gas reserves. His legacy ultimately yielded an army with a state. His "untimely" death—coinciding with a massive drop in oil prices—ushered in a suffocating era of decline.

As the one-party state continued to stagnate, large-scale youth protests broke out, and in October 1988 the army opened fire all over the country. The generals assumed control and, feeling the heat of youth revolt, amended the constitution during a brief "spring" from 1988 to 1991 to allow for multiple political parties. The first open municipal elections in 1991 resulted in a victory by the FIS (Front Islamique du Salut, or Islamic Salvation Front), an Islamist party. Without even allowing a second round of voting, the army generals nullified the elections and aborted the democratic process. Hence was born the term "the Algiers Syndrome," a fear that elections in the Middle East only empower Islamists and that the only defense is dictatorship. The Islamists did not take kindly to the army's diktat and launched a guerilla war. Atrocities perpetrated by both sides killed an estimated 250,000 people, mostly civilians, and disrupted life in every Algerian city and town. Poets, artists, and journalists were among the first targeted by both sides, triggering a mass exodus of the country's intelligentsia, many of whom sought refuge in, of all places, France.

The next essayist describes the violence she witnessed firsthand during the civil war between 1991 and 2000. Her essay brings to light a war often overlooked by Western audiences—a conflict in which violent jihadists and a repressive regime raced to outdo one another in acts of terror and counterterror that disfigured a society otherwise brimming with human potential.

ONE SATURDAY MORNING (THE BEGINNING OF THE WORK WEEK in Algeria), I was running late to elementary school, worried that I might get into trouble for entering the school courtyard just as my classmates were gathering to sing the national anthem. When I walked in, however, I noticed that the melody of the anthem was not in the air, nor the joy that comes with beginning a new day of learning. Instead, students and teachers alike were staring at an ominous-looking poster next to the main entrance. Fear was in the air that sunny day.

The green poster had a chilling message inscribed on it:

The profane French language must be removed from the curriculum.

Proper Islamic garb must be made mandatory for female pupils.

If this decree is not implemented within one week,

we will slaughter you all.

—Front Islamique du Salut

That was a difficult day for everyone at school. At the time, I lived in a neighborhood aptly named the "Red Zone."

My teacher was a beautiful, fair woman, who was brought up in a moderate religious context by preachers associated with the Muslim Scholars' Association. I asked her about the meaning of the message on the poster. She sighed and, in a resigned voice, told us that it was a decision the school would have to implement. "The FIS wants to Arabize and Islamize the new generation and erase the residual impact of the Catholic Church," she explained. The Catholic headmistress of the school, however, was not one to be cowed into changing school policies under threat of violence. She doggedly refused to implement the FIS "decree." And, of course, the FIS—being the FIS—knew no compromise or mercy.

Sure enough, a week later, the headmistress disappeared. We soon learned that she was kidnapped outside her home, taken to a secret location, tortured, and executed. At the same time, our school suffered a terrorist attack that left ten of my classmates dead and many more injured, some permanently.

I was lucky to have avoided physical harm. My family moved to a different neighborhood in Algiers so that I could live and study in a safer environment. That was ten years ago. Yet the images of other children's bodies drenched in blood still haunt me. As does the memory of my headmistress, who endured torture I simply cannot bring myself to describe in writing. (My hands tremble as I type this essay.)

Those of my elders who lived under colonial rule tell me that the French—destructive as they were—were not nearly as brutal as their own compatriots. Some three decades after Algeria was freed from colonial rule, a low-intensity war broke out between the secular, postcolonial regime and radical Islamist groups like the FIS. The war has permanently scarred our young nation. For who can sleep soundly after learning that the Islamic extremists fried children alive to teach their parents a "lesson" in . . . who knows what? (I am reminded of the Qur'anic story of ash-Hab al-Okhdud, in which a group of Muslims is boiled alive simply for believing in the Almighty.) And who can forget that, in one particularly disturbing instance, the Islamists actually gutted twelve of their fellow citizens like sheep at the slaughter, all in the name of "salvation?"

Imagine the fear that was instilled in communities all over Algeria by the relentless kidnappings committed by the FIS and their ideological brethren. They kidnapped the children of wealthy or foreign families to demand exorbitant ransoms. If the families failed to cough up the ransom money, the children would be executed. (And the families would often receive their loved ones' bodies back in pieces.) Tourists were also targeted for kidnapping. Sometimes, they were just killed randomly—as if for sport. Entire villages were terrorized by roving bands who would periodically demand payment from wealthy trader and average citizen alike—or else they faced torture and murder. Tell me, how do these actions comport with Islamic values?

One story from my own neighborhood has stayed with me. The terrorists found an attractive target in an affluent and highly respected family. They forced this family to host them for lunch and give them money. For almost a decade, the family fearfully complied, dutifully wining and dining the unwanted "guests." One day, for no particular reason, the terrorists broke into the house and beheaded every member of the household—man and woman, young and old. How is that for gratitude?

The government often responded with equal brutality. Entire neighborhoods were attacked indiscriminately by the military. Hundreds of innocent civilians—wholly unaffiliated with the FIS—would be killed in these attacks. For a good while, the daily average number of executions hovered around fifteen. Collective massacres carried out by the state were not uncommon.

Sometimes, citizens took the law into their own hands. Recently, the number two leader of the FIS was severely beaten by families of terror victims. The period of "national reconciliation" heralded by the Algerian president has clearly not achieved the desired effect.

The strong people of Algeria, who had endured the hell of French colonial rule, are now being treated to a different kind of terror, inspired by visions of an ideal Islamic state. The terrorists insist that they have noble aspirations, that they kill to bring "salvation" to the Algerian soul. Even so, their methods clearly run contrary to the Islamic worldview. For Islam insists on the legitimacy of the means as much as it cares for the legitimacy of the ends.

CITIZEN OR SUBJECT?

M. Elkhadiri—Morocco—Age 20

In the Western popular imaginary, Morocco is a dream vacation land—a place where one can enjoy the Orient's full exotic potential for a modest fee, along with all of modernity's daily amenities: beautiful resorts, running water, and other pleasures of lesser repute. In the greater game of geopolitics, the Kingdom of Morocco is seen as a staunch Western ally, never failing to demonstrate his friendship with Washington and Brussels—in exchange for financial support and tolerance for the way Morocco handles its internal affairs. Moroccan officialdom never misses an opportunity to point out how "Westernized" their country's foreign policy and market economy are.

When addressing domestic audiences, however, the same officials preface their every statement with the magical phrase that crystallizes Morocco's political realities: "His Majesty, the King, may God grant him victory."

The French retained the ruling Alawi dynasty, which had reigned over Morocco for some four centuries, during their "protectorate" of the North African country. It was a beautifying touch on an otherwise colonial enterprise. At Morocco's independence in 1956, the monarchy was weak and destitute but highly respected by Moroccans as a reminder of a bygone era of national pride and sovereignty. During this early period, through a combination of political maneuvering and brute force, the royal family quickly subdued all attempts to transform it into a constitutional monarchy. Then Crown Prince Hassan II embarked on a remarkably successful power grab.

A larger than life figure, King Hassan II—the Tony Montana of Arab monarchs—quickly neutralized any attempts to limit his power, constitutionally or otherwise. By claiming the title "Commander of the Believers," he consecrated himself, and his issue, as the highest religious authority in the land. This was no coup d'état, but a constitutional act that gave the monarchy a supra-legal status. By virtue of his religious authority, the king simultaneously heads the executive and judicial branches and is not accountable to anyone but himself. In Morocco today—much as in pre-revolutionary France—the state is the king, and the king is the state.

Today, Hassan's son Mohamed VI, a shadow of his late father, retains all the powers his father bestowed on the family. Ministers still bow and kiss the hand of the monarch and his boy crown prince. The king's strong penchant for flashy suits and "business" appetites are by law beyond the reach of his compatriots' criticism. National allegiance to the monarchy is an article of faith. Our next essayist, an educated young Moroccan, is just beginning to question that faith.

"MUHAMMAD, IN FRANCE WE ARE CITIZENS, WHILE YOU MOROC-cans are mere subjects," she said. I was stunned—unable to respond. Nicole was a young French woman who participated in an international youth workshop I also took part in. Her words, uttered while we were informally debating a number of political issues, struck harshly on my ears. I was left humiliated, tempted never to speak with her again.

Days and months after the workshop came to a close and Nicole departed for France, her words still ring in my head. *We are citizens. You are subjects. Citizens. Subjects.* Today, as I look around my city, I cannot help but conclude that Nicole's perspective—as crudely and tactlessly formulated as it was—contains more than a kernel of truth.

I walk past a pack of homeless children in an alleyway. Like street cats, they dine on scraps of food that will undoubtedly damage their health. Their bodies stripped of childish innocence, they stare out from blank faces as if into a vacuum. Their filthy clothes and sad playing "decorate" the streets of poor neighborhoods, but bring little joy. If one were to collapse from hunger tomorrow, the city would be indifferent. Just one less street child to harass passersby for change and a half-eaten sandwich. Who really gives a damn?

We are citizens. You are subjects.

The police and security services are not public servants. They are masters of the public. And if a policeman beats up a youth for looking at him the wrong way, well, that is just how things are. Random violence is the prerogative of the police.

We are citizens. You are subjects.

Students are beaten on campus whenever they speak up for their rights. Their dysfunctional professors receive the same treatment when they protest pay cuts in front of parliament. Anybody invoking the signs of authority, whether by wielding a baton or wearing an ill-fitting suit, is beyond questioning. Security means fear, and the history of repression is deeply rooted in the Moroccan mind.

We are citizens. You are subjects.

Newspapers are daily threatened with closure. The methods the palace deploys to censor dissident voices are becoming ever more cunning. MPs subjected to even the gentlest criticism are free—even encouraged—to bring defamation suits against journalists and intellectuals. Freethinking is a highly proscribed activity.

We are citizens. You are subjects.

Real and imagined threats haunt us. Fear of intelligence ministry officials and security apparatchiks, fear of foreign "subversion," fear of anybody—fear of ourselves! Fear of expressing anger or publicly demanding what constitutes our natural rights. The "fear policy" is infused into Moroccan blood. It is born with the individual, grows with him during primary and secondary school, matures at university, and settles in for the rest of his lifetime. Parents, family members, teachers, professors, policemen—all play their role in maintaining and nurturing it. Although we have made some progress in recent years, finally tearing down the wall of fear itself once and for all has been impossible.

"We are citizens." Will I ever be able respond, "And so are we?"

AT THE POLLING STATION

Abd al-Rahman Khalil—Egypt—Age 20

Throughout his thirty-year reign, Mubarak insisted that his country was a healthy democracy where citizens regularly voted to elect the parliamentary representatives of their choice without state interference. To drive home this theme, Mubarak's own quasi-state party was named—quite inaptly—the "National Democratic Party" (NDP). But dissidents were not under any illusions. For the first twenty-four years of Mubarak's rule, opposition figures were barred from running for the presidency. Rather, Egyptians were asked every six years to participate in national referenda on whether or not they wanted Mubarak to remain president.

In 2005, however, a combination of foreign pressure and growing domestic demand for reform forced Mubarak to allow opponents to run for the presidency. That year, Mubarak was "elected" with a thumping 88.5 percent of the vote—not surprising given massive and well-documented fraud. (After the election, his opponent was hauled off to prison for allegedly forging official documents.) In response, dismayed Egyptians sought refuge in their legendary dark humor. According to a widely circulated joke, "Had Egyptian monitors been asked to resolve the 2000 Florida deadlock between Governor Bush and Vice President Gore, Mubarak would have been elected the forty-third president of the United States!"

In subsequent years, Mubarak attempted to use the NDP as a vehicle for ensuring the succession of his son Gamal to the presidency. This provocative move—in addition to the repeat performance, in 2010, of massive electoral fraud at the parliamentary level—was the straw that broke the proverbial camel's back, setting the stage for the uprising that finally toppled the octogenarian dictator. For the first time in Egyptian history, pharaoh and his heirs stood trial for their legacy of misrule—a development some five millennia in the making.

ON MY TWO-HOUR COMMUTE TO THE UNIVERSITY, I NOTICED A large number of campaign posters for the Egyptian parliamentary elections in the crowded metro car. Everything seemed normal, and a quiet calm surrounded the metro passengers. At the next station, an old man and his young son entered the train and sat beside me. Almost immediately, they began discussing the upcoming elections.

"It seems to me that the Muslim Brotherhood candidate is the best one for our province," the son began. "During the past four years, we never even felt the presence of the National Democratic Party representative. He didn't help my brother get accepted to the Police Academy after they refused him admission just because you . . ." Here, the son hesitated, catching himself mid-sentence only to realize it was too late: "Just because you were a member of the Muslim Brotherhood in your college years."

"Don't assume that a Muslim Brotherhood representative would have intervened on behalf of your brother," the father responded. "Security comes before politics in our country. No member of parliament, no governor will change that. Otherwise, he will be accused of opposing the regime and subsequently lose his seat."

"So you won't cast your vote for the Brotherhood?" the son asked.

"Voting is a waste of time, and not only because the winner is chosen ahead of time," the father said.

The son measured his father's cynicism for a few minutes and decided he was not buying it: "We encourage the system to discriminate against us on the basis of our religious and political affiliations when we stay silent about the crimes committed against us, and because we do not call for our rights," he raised his voice. "As the Prophet Muhammad, peace be upon him, said, 'no right is lost if you demand it,' so I will go to the voting booth and try to change our reality."

The son's reply gave me pause, particularly because the father had been a member of the banned Muslim Brotherhood, participated in its activities, and shared its ambitions against the ruling regime. The way the son gave advice to his father seemed like a passenger on a ship teaching the captain how to navigate. The father smiled calmly and stayed silent, ending the discussion when he noticed many pairs of eyes glaring at them suspiciously.

In the following days, before the election, I struggled to decide whether to insist, like the son, on exercising my democratic rights as an Egyptian citizen, or whether to abstain, like the father, in protest against what are widely seen as sham elections. All the while the son's words and the father's smile were engraved in my mind—both compounding my indecision.

The morning of November 9, 2005, voting day, I skipped classes, deciding instead to head toward the polling station near my house to watch the process. I would leave my decision about whether or not to participate in the elections until after I had witnessed what my fellow citizens looked and sounded like as they fulfilled their civic duty.

I was appalled by what I saw that day. What happened at the polling station had almost nothing to do with civic duty or public service. As soon as the polls opened and lines formed in front of the voting station, people began haggling over the price of votes. "Only 200 pounds?! I heard they vote for 500 pounds in Nasr City," a trader shouted at a vote broker. "I won't sell for less than the market price. No siree!" The broker was having none of it. "500 is too high," he tried to reason. "Prices in poor neighborhoods are not the same as those in wealthy districts." But the trader stood his ground. "That makes zero sense," he quickly retorted. "Here or there, up-down, left-right, the prize is the same—a seat in parliament. And the candidate who pays 500 in Nasr City will not win two seats. A vote is a vote. One man, one vote!" The trader started to back down, and the real negotiation began. "350—no more." "450." "450—that's highway robbery! 375." "400, and I'm offering a real bargain now." "Fine. How many votes do you have?"

I did not vote that day. Instead, I went home, filled with disgust for my fellow Egyptians. How could they cheapen the political process—and themselves—by selling votes? But after giving it some thought, I decided that what the people were doing was perfectly natural. When the outcome of an election is preordained, people anywhere—Egyptian or otherwise—will seek to cash in on the corruption. The father's cynical, world-weary smile prevailed over the son's enthusiasm for justice.

MEMOIRS OF AN EGYPTIAN CITIZEN

Mirette Bahgat—Egypt—Age 25

Egypt, the most populous Arab state with its 82 million inhabitants, is no stranger to elections. For the last sixty years, Egyptians have been hitting the ballot box. But fulfilling their civic duty has had no real impact on Egyptian lives.

Under Egypt's labyrinthine electoral system, with its multiple rounds, votes became a commodity for sale during the successive military regimes. From Nasser to Sadat to Mubarak, vote fraud, either of the ballot-stuffing or the buy-a-vote varieties, deprived elections of their democratic substance. Party bosses, village mayors, and candidates running for elections developed very sophisticated schemes in which districts were distributed between designated "reps" who would each commit to securing a given number of votes. For example, a candidate would pay his "reps" in cash. The reps, in turn, would distribute fruit mixers in their areas on election day and pocket the difference between the "gifts" and the cash they got. The NDP (Mubarak's defunct party) refined these tactics, turning elections into a mere commodities market where the competition was not between ideas and visions of society, but one between domestic appliances brands and cash handouts.

Sadly, Egypt was no exception in terms of electoral fraud; the reality is that most Arab elections in the past decades descended into travesties of democracy. At the end of the day, citizens knew that even if their candidates of choice were elected, they were bound to rubber-stamp parliaments with no real power over the entrenched dictatorial cleptocracies.

I WOKE UP TODAY FILLED WITH JOY. "TODAY I'M GOING TO BE Egyptian for real," I said to myself. Today, I would apply for a voting card to participate in parliamentary elections. Prior to this election cycle, I had not been interested in politics. More recently, however, I had decided that it is my responsibility to have a voice in Egypt's future. My voice must count in how my country is governed, I had concluded.

I knew I was not born into a country with real democracy and transparent institutions. I was well aware of the corruption rampant in Egyptian society and politics. Still, I wanted to at least try and assert my rights.

I went to my room and started gathering the documentation needed for requesting a voting card. I had learned about the process through an awareness campaign launched on Facebook. I imagined myself going to the police station, entering the registration office where a thoughtful official would eagerly be waiting for me. I would carefully complete the application in my best handwriting and hand it to the official, along with the other required documents. I would leave the station elated, reenergized about our country's prospects, and call on my friends to fulfill their civic duty, as well.

I dressed up in my best formal clothes, and off I went with my brother to the nearest police station. On our way, I was singing this beautiful song about Egypt ("Did you see the hope in the eyes of boys and girls? / Did you see people working late to develop their nation?"). I felt very patriotic at this moment; my heart was filled with the love of Egypt. We went through the poor suburbs around Omraneya Street in Giza. I usually hate this impoverished part of town, but today it looked particularly beautiful. I loved the way people looked, recalling Van Gogh's words about the poor: "In the faces of the poor, you can find this hidden beauty, this strong character, that you could never find in the fine faces of tea party ladies."

At last, we arrived at the police station. When we stepped inside, things looked very different from how I had imagined them. I asked the gloomy policeman where we could apply for voting cards. He didn't say a word. He just pointed to the office at the end of the station. There was a large number of people standing in chaotic rows outside the voting office. "At last, the people are starting to take an interest in our civil politics," I thought to myself. "I can just feel that these elections will be different."

I went and took my place in the women's row. Most of the women looked extremely poor, so I was heartened to see them line up for voting. I tried to strike up a conversation with some of the rural women who were standing beside me. "How did you know about the election?" I asked one.

"Um Mohammed came to our street and gathered us to come here and apply," she replied. "She even took copies of our identification to ease the process."

Something inside me wanted to imagine Um Mohammed as a patriotic lady who believed so strongly in democracy that she was compelled to mobilize the community and empower women to vote. But another voice, the voice of logic, was telling me that this was impossible. "And what's her interest in getting you to apply for the voting card?" I asked.

"Well, she gets paid for this," another woman answered. "She gives each of us 30 pounds when we apply and takes the rest of the money." I was shocked. I did not want to believe the words I was hearing—my patriotic dream was turning into a nightmare. I shut my mouth for a while because I felt the women were getting suspicious of me. I was asking too many questions. But I had to know. "Who is Um Mohammed anyway?" I asked, my voice filled with anger. "And where does she get the money from?"

The young women became less suspicious. Now they thought that I, too, was interested in getting my hands on some of Um Mohammed's cash. "She is hired by Doctor Ahmed, from el-Koneisa. He pays her 70 pounds for each voting card," an old woman explained, thinking she was being helpful to another woman in need. "If you can find her, Um Mohammed will give you 30 pounds out of the 70 for registering."

Some civic duty! I wanted to scream in their faces: "Why you do this? Why do you give up your rights? Why do you degrade yourselves?" But I knew they would not understand me. They spoke about this crude mockery of democracy as if it were perfectly normal, a form of charity they receive from the oh-so-compassionate Um Mohammed. They considered their voices so cheap that they would sell them for a mere 30 pounds. What is a "right" anyway? They can only afford to worry about feeding themselves and their children for the day. I looked around me and felt hopeless.

It was getting late, and the row was not moving. Now the policeman was screaming at the "voters," ordering them to step back and stand in a straight line. Like me, he was apparently having a very bad day, albeit for completely different reasons. I noticed two new arrivals standing behind me. While these ladies looked educated, I still suspected that they had come in search of their share of Um Mohammed's money. I glanced in their direction and asked, "Do you intend to vote for someone specific?" They gave me puzzled looks.

"Vote?" one responded. "No, we're just here to apply for the voting card." What the hell? Why would they want to apply for a voting card if they did not intend to use it later? "Well, you see," the other spoke up. "My sister here is getting married, and they told her in church that she can't sign the marital contract without a voting card." Of course! Each institution—including the Coptic Church—has its systems of patronage. These poor ladies were pawns of church politics. That is why they were in line; otherwise, they could care less about voting.

After three hours, I finally got my hands on the application. In my heart, I laughed and cried. I laughed at myself for my naïveté earlier this morning (going into the nice office in the nice police station, meeting the nice employees, and sharing my fellow citizens' pride in Egyptian democracy at work!). I cried at the painful truth.

Was Egypt the same country I was singing for this morning? Had Egypt suddenly turned into such a monstrosity this morning—or had it been this way all along? Was this state of affairs the people's fault? Was it a byproduct of living in ignorance and poverty? No, I could not blame these poor people. They had done nothing to be blamed for; nobody chooses abject poverty. Nor could I blame those of my friends who had left the country years before, having decided they wanted nothing to do with such a place. I could not even reproach my own parents, who had long ago given up participating in elections.

What was I to do? Was I to fight or run away? What if I decided to stay? Is anything going to change? I did not know. My brother was still waiting for his application in the men's line. I noticed he was looking at me pathetically. In my enthusiasm, I had forced him to come along in spite of his reluctance. Now his eyes seemed to pity me while also saying, "I told you so." I did not finish or submit my application that day.

MY MEDAL OF BLASPHEMY

Amr Muhammad an-Nud—Yemen—Age 23

Yemen is a stunted nation, the poster child for Mideast stagnation and decline. As a legacy of British colonialism, Yemen was divided between southern and northern sections. In the south, a leftist elite ushered in a period of relatively stable, albeit Marxist, rule. The north was less "lucky." After removing a medieval imamate in the 1960s, it remained marred in ongoing tribal and sectarian conflict.

North and south rejoined in 1990, but the union failed to bring greater stability, and the country betrayed its ancient Roman moniker of Arabia Felix (happy Arabia). In order to maintain his rule, Yemeni autocrat Ali Abdullah Saleh—in power since 1978—allied himself with every brand of ideological obscurantism and skillfully exploited tribal tensions. His unscrupulous politicking, combined with massive corruption and nepotistic governance, turned Yemen into a failed state.

Three conflicts have rocked the country for years: an ethnic Houthi rebellion in the north, costing thousands of lives; a growing violent crackdown on a popular secessionist movement in the south; and, more recently, an all-out al-Qaeda insurgency owing as much to Saleh's duplicity as to Osama bin Laden's jihad master plan. (Ever since the USS Cole bombing, Saleh has gamed American policymakers, on the one hand pleading his commitment to fighting al-Qaeda while on the other allowing members of his inner circle to assist wanted jihadists—all while deploying fiery anti-Western rhetoric for domestic consumption.)

Yet all this is only half of the story. Leftist rule, at least in the south, left behind residues of cultural progressivism that persist to this day. Meanwhile,

the north has witnessed a mass uprising with millions rallying to demand
Saleh's ouster. The most impressive aspect of this grassroots movement is that,
despite Yemen's being one of the world's most weaponized societies and de-
spite Saleh's brutal repressive tactics, Yemenis have, often though certainly
not always, chosen to shun violence. Even more encouraging, Yemeni demo-
crats organized mass demonstrations to denounce al-Qaeda after it took
over a coastal city, making it clear that they want nothing to do with that
murderous ideology. Alas, young Yemenis' struggle for democracy did not
receive the same media attention in the West as did the revolts in Egypt and
elsewhere.

A FEW MONTHS BEFORE I GRADUATED FROM COLLEGE, A GROUP
of about ninety of my fellow students, both male and female, awarded me
a medal. I had studied diligently during my academic career and had participated in numerous clubs and activities. But the medal I received was not
meant to celebrate my achievements as a student or recognize my extracur-
ricular contributions. It was designed to humiliate me. Inscribed on the
shoddily crafted cardboard "medal" was my name, followed by the words
"BLASPHEMER AND ATHEIST."

Throughout my short life, I had neither blasphemed nor disavowed belief in God. Why, then, were my fellow students compelled to confer this
dubious honor on me? Simply put, it was because I had dared to think differently, to question traditions and orthodoxies, and to speak out against what I
believed—and continue to believe—prevents our small country from moving
forward. In doing so, I crossed crucial red lines and became a threat to the
university establishment.

For example, I completed a senior project investigating reports of physical and sexual abuse inflicted on juvenile offenders entrusted to a certain
state-linked social rehabilitation agency. My findings were shocking. Almost
half of the minors I interviewed reported being subjected to humiliating punishments, including some with sexual undertones, for failing to adhere to a

strict religious code. The degrading practices adopted by its staff stood in stark contrast to the pious values that supposedly inspired the agency's work. When I confronted the agency director with the results of my survey, I was called "morally corrupt" and driven out.

When I reported my findings to my university faculty, I received some support from junior faculty members. But the head of the university, an autocratic professor linked to the ruling party, harshly criticized my research activities. "The organization simply seeks to promote the highest ethical values, in line with our religious teachings, among juvenile offenders," the professor wrote in a letter addressed to me. "Your accusations are simply baseless. I would direct you to conduct research in a different area, and refrain from further investigating this important agency."

Things only got worse when I met with him to discuss the evidence I had uncovered. The professor would neither examine my data nor consider my line of reasoning—his sociology PhD be damned! Finding him unresponsive, I took a more confrontational stance: "Do me a favor, professor," I said. "Spend some time in the care of this organization to see if you would be willing to tolerate for one day what these kids go through for months at a time." Bad move. The professor exploded. His face first turned red, then purple, and he proceeded to hurl every curse word known to our language at me. I walked out of his office, shell-shocked; I had clearly touched a nerve. (Ultimately, I received a mediocre grade on a research project to which I had devoted a great deal of time and energy.)

But my research project was not the only accomplishment that led to my being "awarded" a medal of blasphemy. I also challenged a particularly reactionary Friday prayer leader at the university who consistently espoused extremist views that did not comport with my understanding of our faith. "Your violent rhetoric is out of touch with reality," I told him after one sermon. "It also holds back the faithful and our country." How could he claim that women were the "spit of Satan?" How could he characterize Yemeni women as "immoral entities" who exist to satisfy men's lust but must otherwise be hidden behind walls? And what about his bizarre conception of paradise as a sort of debased pleasure plaza, where the deceased go to eat, drink, and have sex nonstop? Needless to say, the cleric was not amused. In fact, it was the preacher who "inspired" my fellow students to humiliate me with the medal.

The idiotic blasphemy medal aside, my defiance toward those in our society who abuse religion and culture to maintain their hold on power has cost me in more tangible ways. A close family friend, an influential leader in the ruling party, had promised to support me should I seek to enter government service after completing my university education. My activism, however, made him change his mind. "As long as your son continues to criticize the party and the authorities, I will withhold my support from him," he told my father. "Let him taste the bitter flavor of his freedom."

I know full well that the culture of repression is not unique to Yemen but spans whole swaths of the region. Every few years, so-called moderate Arab regimes promise to change the way they govern their societies in order to gain approval from their image-conscious international allies, who in turn provide these regimes with financial support and access to the international economy. For the most part, however, citizens—and particularly dissidents—remain submerged under deep waters of oppression. Once the West stops paying attention, "democratization" and "institution building" are abandoned in favor of good old-fashioned parochialism and repression. Really, it is all akin to a slow, painful death. But hey, at least we are awarded medals for our plight!

THE SHREDDED EXAM CARD

T. T.—Iran—Age 21

The Baha'i are one of the region's most persecuted religious minorities. Founded in nineteenth-century Iran by Baha'u'llah, the Baha'i faith emphasizes the unity of humankind and teaches that all world religions are valid and divine. Since then, the Baha'i have been the subject of a great deal of violence and discrimination in Iran and throughout the region. The Islamic Republic of Iran is particularly threatened by the religion, both because Baha'u'llah's claims of divine revelation come after Muhammad (regarded by Islamic theology as the "last prophet") and because many of the faith's key historic sites are located in Israel.

Under the dictatorial but socially progressive regime of the last Shah, the Baha'i were afforded a great deal of official protection—and thrived as a result. (A Baha'i architect designed Tehran's Freedom Tower—the city's most famous and visible landmark.) Upon deposing the Shah, however, the clerics enacted a vicious and vast complex of discriminatory laws and regulations limiting the rights of Baha'i, particularly with respect to education and social mobility. A confidential 1991 memorandum signed by Seyyed Muhammad Golpaygani, secretary of Iran's Supreme Cultural Revolutionary Council, and approved by the Supreme Leader, spelled out the new regime's education policy toward the Baha'i. The Baha'i, Golpaygani wrote, "must be expelled from universities, either in the admission process or during the course of their studies, once it becomes known that they are Baha'is."

The next essayist is painfully and personally impacted by this vicious policy.

IT ALL BEGAN WHEN MAHBUBEH'S MOTHER TOLD US ABOUT HER daughter's expulsion from the Nemooneh Dolati School, an elite public school in Tehran. That same day, my desire to enter Nemooneh Dolati faded into bitter despair. I felt I had lost all motivation to continue my studies. It was my first encounter with the discrimination surrounding me.

Mahbubeh's expulsion was not an ordinary occurrence. The school officials had explicitly stated their reason for excluding her: she was a Baha'i.

When I was only ten years old, I recognized that our faith set us back in other ways, as well. Around that time, my father was fired from the university where he taught and then permanently banned from teaching. Before being terminated for being a Baha'i, he was one of the top scholars in his field at Shahid Beheshti, the prestigious Tehran academy.

I remember the day my nine-year-old sister's teacher dismissed her from class simply because she was a Baha'i. Shortly thereafter my sister won first place in a province-wide science competition. Only then did a different teacher agree to accept her as one of her students.

I was too young to question why my father could not teach, why my sister got expelled, and why my mother could not be a schoolteacher despite having the required licensure. (Back then, I so wanted to become a teacher myself—a nice teacher, one who would not discriminate against any of her students.)

I put the idea of studying at the Nemooneh Dolati out of my head. I no longer cared to step up my efforts to pass the school's entrance exam. "That's just the way it is. We are Baha'is. Baha'is are not supposed to attend Nemooneh Dolati or any other elite school," I would tell myself. By never asking why, I gained peace of mind.

I entered our neighborhood middle school. Despite all the obstacles placed in my path, I regained my optimism. Although I could not be admitted to Nemooneh Dolati, I hoped that someday I could go to college and continue my studies like everybody else.

Our family friend Zhinus was my inspiration. She was seven years older than me, and everybody admired the way she stuck to her lessons. Even though the Baha'i are banned from college admission, she remained hopeful. Then, something extraordinary happened. That year, she received her national college exam entrance card, one of very few Baha'is to receive one.

She was happy as a clam. She carried on her daily studies more vigorously than ever. She was optimistic and so were we—until the exam day when the security guard shredded her entrance card right before her eyes, simply because she was a Baha'i. All those nights she had spent poring over her books and all those trials and tribulations were nullified in an instant.

Yet Zhinus would not surrender that easily. She took up her studies again, hoping for admission the next year. She remained upbeat until the day the exam cards were distributed. This time they did not even bother to issue her one. There was not even a card to be torn up. Thus Zhinus, who had studied so hard, was deprived of her right to educational advancement.

I tried not to think about her defeat. I had to study. I hoped I could make my father—now dead for eleven years—proud. A father I barely remembered, but who I knew was a kind man whose dreams had been destroyed. I was sure that, in seven years when it would be my turn to participate in the exam, the situation would improve. I hoped I could go to college and compensate for all my relatives who had been denied entrance.

I will never forget the day I saw my name on a banner announcing the winners of an Arabic language olympiad: I had won first place. But my joy was stained by the bitter realization that students who scored below me in the olympiad would advance to the next round, held nationwide, while I was left out.

Being a Baha'i justified this rejection and actually alleviated my sense of indignation.

Days passed quickly. I entered high school. My mother enrolled my sister and me in the city's best school so that her aspirations for us might come true. The school's tuition fees were far more than she could afford, but she wanted the best for her children and longed to see the hardships she had endured for seventeen years pay off through our success.

We went through hard times. I could feel my mother burdened by our school's heavy fees. At the end of every school year, my sister and I would go to the principal and asked to be withdrawn from the school. But the principal would not allow it. She talked about a hopeful future, helping us imagine the day when she would hoist up our names on a flag with all the names of the students headed to college. She, too, believed in us.

I had opted to focus on science studies in high school because I had developed an interest in dentistry. My sister had taken the exam before me, and her ranking was quite admirable. That was the first time in twenty-seven years that Baha'i students could see their test results. However, in the personal information section, "Islam" was printed as the religion field. When it was obvious that my sister could not enter college, I became obsessed with my childhood "whys." Again, the answer was, invariably, *because I am a Baha'i.*

My sister met Zhinus's fate. Now it was my turn. I could not bear to see my feelings get trifled with so easily. Twenty-eight years had passed since the revolution, and during each of those years Baha'i students were banned from moving on to higher education.

My friends' lack of enthusiasm for academics, despite their access to extra tutoring, reminded me of my goals. They studied day and night. One had to study medicine owing to pressure from her family. Another's family forced her to take test prep classes. There were even those who did not want to take the exam at all. Looking at them I would sigh, "I wish I could."

Attending college remains my biggest dream. My greatest aspiration is to make up for everything my mother sacrificed so we might study. I also want to make my father proud.

Yet lately I have felt that my traditional explanations for "why" do not make sense anymore. I now ask: Why shouldn't a Baha'i study? Isn't the right to an education a basic human right? What have people of my faith done to deserve such treatment? Why should a faith that regards all humans as equals—and calls for us all to love one another—deserve this?

I still hope that someday my dream of ending the discrimination, fanaticism, and bigotry will come true because—despite all the hardships—I still believe that where there is faith, hope never dies.

THE EID AL-ADHA BRIBE

Baher Ibrahim—Egypt—Age 21

*On Eid al-Adha, the "festival of sacrifice," Muslims around the world com-
memorate the sparing of Ishmael, Abraham's first-born son, from divinely
ordained sacrifice. For some Muslims, Eid al-Adha is a time to reflect on
Abraham's devotion to God as represented by his willingness to sacrifice his
own son. Others view the Eid as an affirmation of human life. In the next
essay, Baher Ibrahim describes a sacrifice he and his girlfriend had to make
on this most holy day—a sacrifice made not in the name of the divine but
of something sinister and debased.*

*In the essay's social context, premarital relationships between young
men and women are not only taboo but also legally proscribed. Yet—as with
the ban on homosexuality—these restrictions are not uniformly enforced. As
a result, the region's young lovers have been forced to create an entire dating
subculture, daring in its willingness to challenge boundaries but also ever
at risk of being disrupted by the vice police. The essayist offers fascinating
glimpses into Egypt's underground dating scene, as well as the bizarre morality "economy"—built on the most sanctimonious piety but sustained by
threats and bribes.*

MUCH INK HAS BEEN SPILLED REGARDING THE TRAGIC STATE OF
civil rights in my country. Press censorship, vote tampering, police brutality,
and arbitrary detention have all been the subject of much critical scrutiny by

Egyptian liberals. The repression of civil and political rights is crystal clear for all to see and is indeed a very significant issue. However, I will describe a painful personal experience of mine that highlights the repression of a much more basic freedom that is forcibly usurped from all Egyptians—a right so basic that people in much of the world take it for granted.

It was a winter night, which happened to coincide with the feast of Eid al-Adha. My girlfriend and I were walking hand-in-hand in the Montazah Palace Gardens of Alexandria. The weather was cool and crisp and the mood was festive. Songs were playing, and children were running around in their best Eid clothes. Romance was in the air as we expressed our love for each other and lamented the society that would not let us love each other in peace. I was intoxicated by the sweet fragrance of the gardens.

"When will we be able to be together without attracting those holier-than-thou, accusatory stares everywhere we go?" I whispered to her. "I love you and I want nothing more than to be with you."

I had heard her response many times before: "I love you too, but what can we do? This is how things are done in Egypt. If we were in America, we'd be living on our own terms. We'd just get married and live together, pure and simple. Here, I have to be a 'good girl' until we are old enough to be officially involved—and until you have enough money."

"We are nineteen. How old do we have to be to take control of our own feelings? Are we really expected to wait twenty years until I've made enough money?" I let out a sigh of despair and kissed her hand.

We had arrived at a large green enclosure, full of tall trees. There were no lamps around the trees. The soft glow of the moonlight was enchanting.

I slowed down, still clasping my beloved's hand tightly, my body and soul exuding affection for this one other being. A quick glance revealed that we were not alone. At the foot of nearly every tree, there was a young couple sitting in the semidarkness. Some were holding hands, some were cuddling, and others were whispering what were probably vows of devotion and love. Without thinking about it, it was easy to tell that they were all like us: unmarried, rejected by society, and in financial straits.

A huge tree trunk beckoned me to sit at its massive base, under its network of infinite branches and leaves. I could not resist. This was a chance to sit in privacy away from prying eyes and intruders. I glanced at my girlfriend. She understood my signal and silently complied. We got off the main road and wandered in between the trees, leaves and twigs cracking underneath our feet. Many young couples were on either side of us, all too in love to notice. My heart was pounding, and my sweetheart could feel my racing pulse. Eventually we reached a secluded tree at the center. We both sat down in silence. Our motions mingled together in perfect symmetry as I placed my arm around her shoulder. It was so quiet. My breathing sounded like a symphony.

I don't know how long we stayed there, but it could not have been long. We spoke of the difficulties we faced. How could we get married without the money to pay for an Egyptian wedding? Why was everyone judging us as if we were immoral criminals? What were we doing wrong? Is it so wrong for two souls living in a country that breeds despair to find happiness in one another? I leaned by head toward her and rested it on her shoulder and closed my eyes.

Suddenly, our solace was shattered into a million pieces by a sinister voice that pierced the silence like a bullet. "Your ID card, now!" I felt a hand land softly on my shoulder as a voice that smelled of cigarettes barked, "Come with me!"

I had seen this happen in movies but never thought it would happen to us. I didn't need to ask who he was; I knew he was a thug employed by the morality police. He led us into an entirely secluded area at the periphery of the garden and spoke slowly and softly to torture us mentally. It had never occurred to me that the men charged with policing prostitutes and brothels would be threatening two innocent people with arrest and scandal.

The vice cop stood inches away from us, blowing cigarette smoke in our faces. We were terrified, and he knew it. I was about to simultaneously faint and explode from fear. His threats came out in slow motion.

"You know that you two have committed a grave offense," he calmly explained. "Committing an indecent act in a public place is against the law.

Do you know that I am supposed to arrest both of you now and take you to the police station?"

The words "police station" crippled me. Only God knew what would happen to me if we were detained overnight. I had heard hundreds of tales about women who were raped and abused while in detention—what would become of my lover? If we were arrested, it would be the end of everything: our relationship, our reputations, our parents' trust in us. We would have a criminal record that would haunt us all our lives. My knees were shaking as I struggled to form audible sentences.

"Isn't there any other way to do this?" I groveled. "Please, sir, we are young. This girl is my fiancée. We recited the first chapter of the Qur'an just today, and our parents allowed us to go out alone for the first time. We didn't know we were doing anything wrong! There were lots of people by the trees!"

I said all this in one breath and it left me gasping for air. My head was on fire despite the winter breeze. My girlfriend was silent through the whole ordeal. The sinister creature motioned for me to walk a few feet away till she was out of earshot. He sat down lazily on a rock and casually lit another cigarette, even offering me one for dramatic effect. Then his demeanor suddenly changed, and I knew that arresting us was the last thing on his mind. He played his part for what must have been the millionth time, taking sadistic pleasure in my fear.

"What do you want me to do? I can't just leave you." He was almost friendly now. "If I could let you go, I would. But the problem is my commanding officer. We've already arrested a truckload of you young punks." Then, after a beat during which he switched his glance to the ground: "The officer would be willing to let you go, but not for free. Everyone has his weaknesses."

I was too scared to mention the money he was obviously asking for, so I waited until he set a price of fifty pounds. I paid it gladly, and he resumed his contemptuous tone, telling us to get lost. I thanked him and told him that God would reward him in the afterlife.

That was the first bribe I had ever paid in my life, but it was not the last. It was a bribe I was forced to pay because we young Egyptians are denied our most basic right: the right to express our feelings, the right to be sincere. The most basic emotions cannot be expressed without risking punishment. Two people with no hope in sight are forbidden by a tyrannical government from loving each other. A corrupt leadership has robbed the Egyptian people of the only thing left that distinguishes them from inanimate objects: their feelings.

My dream deferred is a country where love is not forbidden. Love not only in the romantic sense. But love for our neighbors, for our co-workers, for our leaders, and for our country. Because if we cannot love each other, we might as well die.

THE TRAGEDY OF MY LOVER

S.B.—Morocco—Age 22

Moroccan society challenges perceptions of what "Muslimness" is about. The common sight of a young woman in shorts on a moped (perhaps with her mother veiled from head to toe in the back seat) riding down a busy street in Marrakech raises a thought-provoking question: How can a young woman trump basic Islamic precepts in broad daylight in a Muslim nation?

As it is, the accepted narrative about Muslims breaks the global community of adherents to that faith into two neat categories: (1) traditionalists, seen as the "authentic" Muslims who abstain from alcohol or pork consumption, dress conservatively, and so on, and (2) moderate, "inauthentic" Muslims, who adopt Western norms and attitudes and who do not represent their societies.

Homosexuality shatters this narrative. Both "authentic" and "moderate" Muslims would generally reject and denounce homosexuality. Yet, gay men and lesbians in the Middle East and North Africa populate both categories. Some are religiously devout despite the clear Islamic prohibition of homosexuality. Others are "moderates" who, by dint of their sexual orientation, would still be shoved right back into the closet—if not worse—by their fellow "moderates."

In Morocco as elsewhere in the region, traditionalist social norms and state repression join forces to target the most vulnerable social group: members of the Mideast's LGBT communities. Homosexuality is officially a crime in Morocco, and many families disown their gay and lesbian relatives. Nevertheless, as in all countries across the region, a gay subculture persists in Morocco. Gay Moroccans have a heavy online presence, and their pickup spots and dating scenes are sometimes tolerated by the monarchy—despite the latter's status as guarantor of the Muslim faith. There are even openly gay publications and associations in the kingdom and across the region.

While dealing with the sensitive subject of homosexuality in the Muslim world, the next essay also echoes the tales of star-crossed lovers so common in Arabic and Persian storytelling. The Mideast's classical literature brims with stories of lovers prevented from reaching each other—by family, society, and fate itself. Yet there is nothing exotic about the searing account of forbidden love that follows, as the essayist brings the human cost associated with the region's homophobic laws and attitudes into stark relief.

WHERE AND HOW DO I BEGIN? WHEN YOU FAIL TO FACE DESTINY, when you are only left with grief, when the entire world goes dark, rational thought becomes difficult. You ask naïvely and in vain, "What happened?" and "How did it happen?" Conflicting feelings overwhelm you, a fever runs through your body, colorless images ceaselessly play in your mind, you sigh deeply, and you look around angrily. You speak to yourself like a raving lunatic. Finally, you spit on life and on yourself. This is how I feel every time I recall the story of Esam.

Esam was born into an impoverished family in the city of Agadir in southern Morocco. His family was deeply pious, and he was required to adhere strictly to the religious mores. Esam's father, Cid Abdulkader, was a tyrannical man who ruled his family with an iron fist. Nobody could stand in his way or question any decision he made. Esam was three months older than me, and his house was next door to mine. We knew each other from early childhood and went to school together. We were the best of pals. (I remember being devastated when I heard that his father beat Esam every time we played together. To Cid Abdulkader, playing was a crime.)

As the years went by, Esam and I began discussing the changes our bodies were undergoing. We shared our most intimate desires. At fifteen, we had sex. At first we did not give it much thought—we just slept together. But eventually, the faint feelings of guilt started to mar our enjoyment. We knew what we were doing was "wrong" because we had always been taught that only men and women can have sex, and then only after marriage. Our actions disgusted us. Our families would surely disapprove—and so would God. Men were made for women—not for each other. And yet, we kept on having sex—promising ourselves that each encounter would be the last. Try as we might to avoid each other for as long as we could, we would find ourselves back in each other's embrace in no time.

When Esam turned eighteen, however, he started to avoid me. It seemed as though the pious austerity ingrained in him ever since he was a child had finally awoken. He refused my advances, brushing my hand away when I tried to hold his. He warned me about the great and eternal punishment that awaited those who, like us, had sex with the same gender. When I insisted, he ended our friendship altogether. "You are manipulating me to satisfy your own filthy desires," he sneered at me contemptuously. "You disgust me."

His transformation was difficult to bear. He was my only friend. And more than that, he was my lover. Every time I tried to expel him from my heart, my love for him only grew stronger. Perhaps I was lucky to move to Casablanca after graduating from high school. There, I studied engineering at university. Esam stayed in Agadir to work as an agricultural technician after a brief stint at trade school. We did not see much of each other for a while, except during holiday breaks.

Then one day, Esam contacted me in Casablanca. "I have to see you," he told me over the telephone. And sure enough, he showed up on my campus a fortnight later. We went for a stroll on the beach. I could immediately tell that Esam's demeanor had changed—yet again. To my delight, he had once again assumed his charming, friendly persona. We were discussing old times when, suddenly, he grabbed and held my hand. He tried to speak but could not find the words he was looking for. "What is it, *habibi?* Tell me." I became worried.

"I . . . I . . . I . . ." Still, he could not speak.

I became furious. "What is it, for God's sake? Are you having trouble with your father, at your job? Do you need money? Just get it out!"

He looked into my eyes, and then embraced me tightly. "I love you, S.," Esam whispered in my ear. "I tried, I tried to stay away from you but I could not. I was torn between you and my conscience." Then: "My love for you is wrong, but I cannot fight it."

He continued speaking, but I do not recall the rest of his words. I just kept staring into his eyes and sobbing. I wanted to cry out my love for him right then and there but could not. I was overcome with bliss. That was the happiest night of my life.

With great difficulty, Esam and I parted ways for the time being. He went back to his farming while I returned to my studies. I felt I could face the world with renewed confidence. My lover was back in my life, and our relationship had only grown stronger. We called each other every night, flirting and exchanging "I-love-yous."

But it was not meant to be. The next summer, Esam's father chose a wife for him, his cousin, who he was suddenly forced to marry. I was left shattered and heartbroken and decided I would never go back to Agadir. I hated that city and I hated Cid Abdulkader. Maybe I even hated Esam, who still called me and sent me e-mails regularly. When I heard his voice on the phone, I would listen for a few seconds—then hang up. His e-mails aroused my pity. He described how he felt stuck in a loveless marriage with a woman he did not and could not love. He was gay right down to his very soul, yet he was forced to maintain the pretense of heterosexual love. Even so, I never responded to his e-mails. I still blamed him for accepting the arrangement. When my anger subsided, I asked myself what I would do were I faced with the same quandary. I would do the same thing, I concluded. And so I began taking Esam's calls and responding to his e-mails.

Then the e-mails stopped coming. So did the calls. I grew worried, but told myself that this was only the natural course of events. Esam was husband to a wife. He no longer had time for our love. Months went by, and another summer came. One morning, my dorm room telephone rang. It was my sister. She sounded sad. I immediately knew something was terribly wrong. "Esam is dead. He committed suicide." I dropped the receiver. My legs went numb. I went dizzy. I collapsed. "Esam is dead, Esam is dead," my sister's voice kept echoing in my skull.

When I went back to Agadir, the neighborhood was in disarray. From the accounts offered by his colleagues and friends, I put the pieces of the puzzle together. Apparently, Esam had been surfing a gay website during one of his breaks, not realizing that his boss was standing behind him looking at the computer monitor. There was no explaining the situation on Esam's part, no way to justify himself. He was fired on the spot and driven out of the building. Then word spread around the neighborhood at lightning speed. When his wife learned that her husband was gay, she immediately asked for a divorce. His family disowned him for good. Soon after, Esam drowned himself in the sea.

At his funeral, I kept wishing I had had the courage to do the same thing so I could join my lover in death. What crime had he committed to be treated that way? I bade him farewell and left Agadir as soon as possible—I could not stay among so many hypocrites. When I arrived back in Casablanca, I found a letter from Esam waiting for me:

S., my love:

I do not know what I have done to deserve being abandoned by my own family. I had always been an obedient son. I treated young and old with kindness and respect. I did not choose to be homosexual; I was made this way. So why would they treat me like that? I even accepted a forced marriage just to please my father. After losing my job, I was treated as an outcast by my own loved ones. By the time you read this letter, I will have left this world. My hope is in you, S. My hope is that you will fight this injustice.

Your Esam

Esam was twenty-four years old when he killed himself. The injustice he spoke of in his suicide note goes far beyond the actions of a tyrannical father or a gossipy neighborhood. It is enshrined in the notorious item "489" of Moroccan law, which criminalizes homosexuality. Discrimination against gay men, men like me, is an everyday norm taken for granted in Morocco today. The abuses are too many to keep track of. Advocacy groups and NGOs working on this issue are under constant pressure from the state. I am determined to carry out my lover's last wish, but LGBT activists here face an uphill road. And Esam is out at sea.

ART IN A CAGE

Taha Belal—Egypt—Age 22

Taha Belal is an accomplished young Egyptian artist working in mixed media whose work juxtaposes cutouts from newspapers in different languages and other everyday objects and images in startling fashion. Belal seeks to explore the instability of meaning in the age of globalization and information technology. "In making the work I am consistently confronted with information's superficiality and meaninglessness," he says in an artist statement. "My grasp begins to slip. I am both drawn to and repulsed by these objects; I revel in the instant of seeing something I can relate to, and I recognize something arrested, and I seek to extend that moment. Simultaneously, however, I am thrown off by its inherent instability, and inevitably all I am left with is image/surface."

Belal returned to his native Egypt after completing his undergraduate education in the United States. His essay, written in the aftermath of the Danish cartoon controversy, places him in the shoes of an insider looking at his own society from the outside. Eager to create art that interrogates and actively intervenes in its social context, Belal is shocked to find an Egyptian art scene floundering after decades of censorship and repression.

RECENTLY, THE WORLD CAUGHT A GLIMPSE OF THE GLOBAL BATtle for individual rights in the events that followed the publication by several European newspapers of controversial cartoons depicting the Prophet

Mohammed. Protests throughout the Muslim world erupted, flags were burned, and embassies were attacked. But the European newspapers stood firm in defiance. Publishing the cartoons, they insisted, was their right under Europe's free-speech laws and traditions. Many Muslims, however, saw the cartoons as blasphemous and insulting to Islam. The cartoon controversy reflects the stark difference in values between the West and the Muslim world when it comes to freedom of speech and expression.

As a Muslim artist, I am convinced that our societies, particularly those in the Mideast, must be willing to look long and hard at our own mindsets and to reexamine our basic assumptions. In the Mideast, many forms of expression, ranging from sexual to religious, are forbidden. It is high time for drastic change. The region desperately needs to free itself from the shackles of stagnation and finally become part of the free world. The Muslim Mideast has the potential to once again foster free thinking, stimulate creative growth, and provide a culturally rich environment that supports development.

I did not always view things along these lines. It was only after I had the opportunity to study art in the United States and to experience Western culture first-hand that I realized the need to scrutinize my own identity and beliefs. Once granted free reign to explore, my artwork touched on a variety of identity issues such as politics, language, and culture; much of my work also dealt with sensitive and taboo subjects such as sexuality and faith.

After completing my undergraduate degree in fine arts at an American university, I returned home to Cairo. I knew it would be difficult to exhibit my work in Egypt. My art deliberately treaded in taboo areas and crossed lines. Nevertheless, I decided to research exhibition opportunities. Previously, I had seen several exhibitions at a gallery, one of the few exhibition spaces independent of the regime, dedicated to showing contemporary artwork. Portfolio in tow, I paid the director a visit. After looking at my portfolio, the director told me that while some of my pieces could narrowly escape government scrutiny, the rest were simply impossible to display.

To prove his point, the director cited an instance where the gallery had been forced to close an exhibition that was seen as blasphemous by the gov-

ernment. Even after the gallery won a court case, the artwork remained confiscated. I was also shown a secret exhibition catalog hidden away in one of
the director's drawers. It was the work of a Lebanese artist who had previously
exhibited at the gallery many times. But this particular series of paintings,
which criticized certain aspects of Islam, could only be exhibited abroad with
no Cairo publicity.

The meeting quickly brought me to my senses. I was not about to risk
my career and potentially my liberty to exhibit my US portfolio. I also realized just how perilous is the position of Egyptian artists. My years abroad had
made it easy to forget the censorship machine at home. Later that summer, I
showed an artist friend of mine some of my most recent work. His response
was the same: I could forget about exhibiting the work in Egypt. He also
mentioned that it would be a good idea not to show the work to anyone else.
I was reminded of an Egyptian artist quoted in Douglas Kennedy's book on
the Egyptian art scene, *Beyond the Pyramids* (which, by the way, is banned in
Egypt). The artist explains that although an artist may be able to create what
she wants within the confines of a more closed society, "the problem is that,
in Egypt, you make what you want inside a cage."

My realization was reinforced by the quality of the art that was approved
for exhibition by the regime. Much of it was mundane, uninteresting, and
far from thought provoking. In exhibitions such as the annual Youth Salon,
ostensibly showcasing some of Egypt's finest young and emerging artists, I
found nothing but mediocrity and conformity. The artists represented all
hovered around the same ideas. At best, they flirted with the boundaries—
but they never came close to breaking through or going over the edge. This
was art as decoration at its worst.

The grand Cairo Biennial, which is marketed as "the biggest international exhibition in the Arab world," was similarly underwhelming. *Art in
America*'s Lilly Wei hit the nail on the head, describing the exhibit as a terrific opportunity wasted on "dated, uninspired, provincial work with almost
nothing that stood out." It was the same story at the recently re-inaugurated
Museum of Modern Art in Cairo, where most of the work never strayed from
landscapes or tame abstractions.

Censorship has deprived Middle Eastern societies of artists' voices. Whether by force or by choice, well-established artists such as Shirin Neshat from Iran and Ghada Amer from Egypt currently live abroad. Both are critically engaged with major Middle Eastern cultural issues such as gender inequity within Islam, but they cannot reach the audience that could really benefit from critical engagement with their creations. I fear that my voice and ideas will also be kept away. Although the censorship of art is only part of the greater problem that societies in the Middle East face today, it is nonetheless a clear reflection of the broader reality.

BLACK LIKE ME

Sameer az-Zein—Sudan—Age 24

Racism in the Middle East, particularly that targeting black Africans, is not openly discussed. For centuries, Arab militias raided African villages, and a network of merchants transported captured slaves via Saharan caravans or by boat throughout the Persian Gulf. Slave markets operated openly in Morocco, Libya, Syria, and Oman into the twentieth century (Saudi Arabia did not formally outlaw slavery until the 1960s). Because it was colonial powers that largely stamped out the slave trade by force, no strong indigenous abolitionist movement emerged to work toward racial reconciliation.

Black slavery today remains a muted memory in most Middle Eastern countries—with the exception of Sudan and Mauritania. Racial tensions lie at the heart of Sudanese identity. The country—whose name derives from the Arabic "Bilad as-Sudan," literally, "land of the blacks"—has witnessed centuries of raids by Arab slave traders against indigenous Africans. Over time, a dual process of Arabization and Islamization has transformed the country, so that many Sudanese today consider themselves Arab Muslims despite their dark skin pigmentation. Yet brutal conflicts in Darfur and southern Sudan, which recently declared its independence from the genocidal regime in Khartoum, offer a stark reminder that there are large minorities of Sudanese who refuse to relinquish their African and/or non-Muslim identities.

Beyond Sudan, racial tensions simmer across the region in subtler ways. Darker-skinned Arabs feel racially disparaged when their fellow, lighter-skinned Arabs use derogatory terms such as "Abeed," meaning slaves— official ideologies of Arab brotherhood and solidarity notwithstanding.

Unofficially, the Arab world is too often divided between "class-A" Arabs with whiter skins and dark-skinned "class-B" Arabs, who hail from North Africa or are descendants of slaves. A black Sudanese Muslim, our next essayist finds himself at the intersection of these turbulent racial fault lines.

AS I WRITE THIS (IN 2009), THE RULING REGIME IN KHARTOUM—which has ideological ties to the Muslim Brotherhood—is preparing to mark the twentieth anniversary of the coup d'état that brought it to power. There is little to celebrate about the National Islamic Front's almost two decades in power. The regime's use of racial and tribal discrimination to prolong its longevity has led to racial violence. Sudan has earned international ignominy for its cruel policies toward its black citizens, particularly in the south.

My earliest memory of racial repression in Sudan involves my time at an elementary school set up by the Catholic Church to serve the needs of children displaced and orphaned by Sudan's civil wars. Father Daniel Comboni, a kindly priest who genuinely cared about each and every one of his young wards, ran the school. He offered us a brief respite from the constant violence that had shaped our childhoods. He offered us the opportunity to learn and—a rarity for Sudan—to be children. Not long after my arrival, however, regime officials closed down the school, claiming that Father Comboni was using it as a platform to proselytize among Muslim children. This was a shameful lie. In fact, Father Comboni had hired a Qur'an teacher to instruct us in the basic tenets of our religion. Missionary activity was not tolerated in his school.

We were devastated by the closure of the school, and particularly insulted by the false accusations lodged against Father Comboni. The fact of the matter was that the school was catering to the needs of a persecuted racial minority in Sudan. And the regime could not afford us even this small measure of happiness and opportunity.

Even so, I made my way through the educational system, eventually graduating from high school. When I did, I immediately applied to the military academy in the hope of becoming an engineer with the rank of first lieutenant. There was no way I could afford a private education. The state-financed military academy offered someone from my background the only chance at higher education and social mobility.

My application proceeded swimmingly through the initial stages. I had high grades and easily passed the medical and security screenings. I was among the top candidates. But once again, the discriminatory policies of the state stood in my way. The director of admissions disdained applicants with black African origins, particularly those, like me, who had not joined pro-party student organizations during their high school years.

My hopes of earning a college education dashed, I joined the swelling ranks of unemployed and underemployed young Sudanese. For many of us, especially the blacks, escaping Sudan now represents the only hope for a better life. Many look to Israel, of all places, as a possible refuge—an oasis of peace and prosperity. But getting there is not so easy. Often, Africans on their way to the Jewish state are arrested and even killed at the Egyptian border. (This has led one of our communal leaders, Alsayed Abdel Wahed Mohammed Nour, to open an office in Tel Aviv to advocate for the rights of Sudanese refugees.)

Sudanese of African origin are viewed as dangerous "others" by the state and by the Arab majority. We have become aliens in our own land. So the state-sponsored celebrations in the coming days will only leave us nauseated, reminding us of our negation by the state—and by our fellow Muslims.

PART II

UNEQUAL

"The bird was truly free."

—Forough Farrokhzad

A PERSIAN GRANDMOTHER IN TOKYO

B.A.—Iran—Age 20

The clerical regime that rode a wave of popular anger to power in Iran's 1979 revolution claims to be divinely inspired and to derive legitimacy from Islam itself. The Iranian constitution vests absolute power in a supreme jurisconsult who controls the major organs of state power (the military, judiciary, and state-run media) and can nullify the actions of the "popular" branches of government. Iran's penal code, based on Islamic law, targets dissidents, ethno-sectarian minorities, and LGBT Iranians.

Iranian law also relegates women to second-class status. Women are forced to veil themselves in public, cannot travel unaccompanied by a male guardian, and are barred from running for president. A woman's testimony is worth half that of a man's in court, as is her parental inheritance.

Since the early days of the Islamic Republic, Iranian women have fought to dismantle the regime's system of gender apartheid. Early on, such resistance took the form of forceful, if unsuccessful, rallies against compulsory veiling. More recently, Iranian women have launched mass mobilization campaigns, such as the "One Million Signatures" campaign challenging apartheid laws. As our next essayist demonstrates, for many young Iranian feminists, the courageous older women in their own families often provide that first activist spark.

MY PARENTS DIVORCED WHEN I WAS TWO. MY FATHER WENT TO India to continue his university studies, and my mother went back to her hometown in the provinces. I was put in the care of my paternal grand-parents, who lived in Nezam Abad, one of Tehran's poorest districts. When I turned seven, I started attending a public school near my grandparents' house. It was during this time that my little brain became host to all kinds of strange musings and funny dreams. Maman—as I called my grandmother—was the only one willing to lend an ear to my naïve curiosities.

Father's was a large family. My grandparents had seven children, my father being their second. Most of my aunts and uncles had married. They all called my grandmother "Abji." (I was the only one who called her Maman.) She was my best friend during those years of happy solitude. Maman, or Abji, could not read or write. She was a pious woman, meticulous about her daily prayers, fasts, and rituals. I naturally adopted her spiritual perspective on life.

In the second grade, my teacher insisted that we memorize the names of all twelve saints, or imams, of the Shi'a faith. Like many of my classmates, I had the hardest time with this particular assignment. Back at home, no matter how hard I tried, I could not cram these sacred names into my tiny head. My practice recitations went something like this: "Ali . . . Hassan . . . Hussein . . . Zein al-'Abidin . . ." Then came the fifth imam, whose name was a permanent stumbling block!

Finally, I ran crying to Maman. "I just can't remember them!" I wailed.

"Remember what, dear?" Maman asked.

"The names of the imams," I explained tearfully. "We have to memorize all twelve for tomorrow's class."

"May dirt fall on their heads!" Maman replied, using the phrase she reserved for when she was most angry. "The things they make you poor kids do at such a young age!"

After fuming for a bit, Maman began to console me. "It's all right, dear, we'll figure something out. . . . You remember the first three, right?" "Yup." "And what about the fourth imam, the one who fell ill and died, you remember his name too, right?" "Yes." When we reached the fifth imam, Bagher al-Ulum, Maman came up with an amusing memorization strategy. "Try to remember him with *gher*," she said. "We *gher* when we dance, right?" We burst out laughing. She had made a hilariously inappropriate pun. "Ba" in

Persian means "with." And "gher" is the word we use to describe the seductive hip swings and gyrations that define Persian dancing. Ba-gher! With the help of Maman's racy puns and cheerleading propelling me forward, I managed to memorize all twelve names in no time. And come to think of it now, the poor woman had probably managed to learn these names using the same "methods."

A year or so later, the teachers at the same school told us that we were about to reach the state of *bolough,* or sexual maturity. We were ready to be wed, according to religious doctrine. "We must get ready for your 'duty ceremony,'" the principal announced at a school assembly. "Tell yours parents to buy you angel-white dresses."

"What's *bolough?*" I asked Maman when I got home. "You are too young to know about these things." She brushed my question off but promised to speak with the principal. Though I was ultimately forced to participate in the ceremony, I learned years later that Maman had indeed given the principal a piece of her mind: "*Bolough* ceremonies were something they did in the years of yore when they would make thirteen-year-old girls put on wedding gowns," she had yelled. "*Don't you dare fill my granddaughter's head with such claptrap!*"

While Maman was seemingly a mere illiterate, I learned so much from her. She knew that civil law and Shari'a are two separate spheres. Like many women of her generation, she intuitively understood that faith should not be mixed with worldly laws and politics. Maman, although a woman of deep faith, was convinced that one's relationship with God should be strictly a matter of the heart.

After high school, my father—who had married a Japanese woman in India and was now living in Japan—offered me the opportunity to attend college in Tokyo. I accepted. During the winter of 2007, my father invited my grandparents to visit Tokyo. I was elated. It was the first time Grandpa had been out of the country although Maman had gone to India with me to visit Father several times and had also made pilgrimages to Mecca and the shrine of Sayyida Zainab in Damascus. Still, this was the first time my grandparents were experiencing an advanced industrial, fully democratic society.

They were astonished. Everything seemed new and surreal to them. But my grandfather, who had been a religious man all his life, was not too shocked by the sights in Tokyo to forgo his religious duties. When he could not find the direction of Mecca, my father helped him, and the two prayed together.

Given how difficult it was for her to walk to begin with, using the escalators and the subway were the main problems Maman faced in Tokyo. But she, too, was dazed by the city around her. After visiting a lot of tourist attractions in Japan and meeting many Japanese, one day Maman asked me: "Dear, are all these people Muslims?"

I smiled and replied: "Maman, most of them don't have any particular faith."

"You mean they are infidels?"

"Not in the sense you mean."

She thought about my response for a few minutes. "For so many years, we'd been hoping for paradise in the next world, while these infidels have created their own heaven on earth," she mused.

WANTED FOR FINDING INSPIRATION IN JAPAN

This young Iranian writer, who goes by "B.A." for her own safety, recently won second prize in the Dream Deferred essay contest. Her essay describes the complex relationship with her grandmother and an eye-opening travel experience they shared in Japan. In the following interview from 2009, B.A. talks about viewing Iran from abroad and the promise her grandmother represents for one day reconciling modernity and tradition.

Your essay explores how experiences traveling outside Iran have given you insight into your own society. Can you give an example?
As a child, I frequently traveled to India. On one such trip, I remember visiting the Jame Mosque in New Delhi. Surrounding the mosque were homeless Muslims living in poor conditions. I asked my father how this could be. He

said, "If we Muslims around the world cannot change our view on modernity and technology and learn to live harmoniously with people of other religions, we will not progress and develop!"

You describe your grandmother visiting Japan and
calling it "their own heaven on earth." Why did
you end your essay with this observation?

My grandmother's visit to Japan not only reaffirmed her faith, but also made her ask more from its followers. How could a non-Muslim country like Japan achieve such progress and development? She wants and expects more from her fellow Muslims, believing that if they can recreate their own heaven on earth, they will have one waiting for them in the next life. Her experiences helped her realize there is something to learn from anyone and everyone, and that fostering diversity and acceptance is important to a community's success.

How has visiting Japan changed your view of Iran?

In Iran, any time we tried to talk about our freedoms and rights under civil law, we were told by the authorities: "What you want is unrestrained and undisciplined wildness, not freedom." They invoke religion as a tool to deny us basic rights. But in Japan people enjoy freedom without wildness. People respect social rules but are also free to be themselves. I ask myself how many years it will take for Iran to be like this. At the same time, I was in Tokyo during the recent postelection protests in Tehran. It was great to see Iranians in Japan demonstrating against the regime's repression. I was proud, as an Iranian, to see this struggle for freedom.

BREAKING NEWS: MP REVEALS HERSELF AS BANNED POET

H.H.—Egypt—Age 20

Women in the Middle East face discrimination arising from both social mores and religious dogma. An even more daunting challenge is the one posed to lesbians in the region. Those from the upper echelons of some Mideast societies may find a degree of space underground to express their orientation. The rest, however, are condemned to the closet. The common thread in the entire region is that under no circumstance will a woman be allowed to openly state her gay orientation. Were a woman to come out, the state response would vary from country to country: flogging in Iran (where gay men must choose between forced sex reassignment and execution); "corrective rape" in Sudan; prison in Egypt; a death sentence in Saudi Arabia. In some countries, families marry off young lesbians to preempt any "dishonor," with the first child serving as incontrovertible biological proof of intact honor.

Middle Easterners often claim that homosexuality is not part of the region's culture. Islamists go further, arguing that it is a Western perversion designed to subvert Muslim culture. (Christians in the region also often express similar sentiments, by the way.) What very few people in the region would admit is that homosexuality has been pervasive throughout their histories, including early Islamic history. For example, the eighth-century Baghdad poet Abu Nawwas openly proclaimed his homosexuality in his verse. While some of Abu Nawwas's poems are mandatory reading in Arab school curricula as exemplars of the "wineries genre," seldom is he presented as a gay man. Abu Nawwas's ultimate demise was the work of the religious establishment, the very institution in whose name gays are still persecuted

*in the region. Picking up where Abu Nawwas left off twelve centuries ago,
our next essayist confronts the same forces of repression head-on in her mock
news report. The first thing to note about the essay is the extent to which its
vision of an Egyptian woman—a member of parliament, no less—bravely
coming out of the closet is, in fact, a complete fantasy. That the incidents
related by our "reporter" seem so implausible is telling of the dismal state of
LGBT and—by extension—women's rights in the Mideast.*

*"H.H." has also written one of the more subversive essays in the anthology. Set in 2014, the article contains a story within a story, or, to be more
precise, a poem within a mock news story. The lesbian MP at the heart of the
piece is supposedly the author of* Reading the Qur'an in Lesbos—*a provocative book of poems. That title alludes to* Reading Lolita in Tehran, *a bestselling memoir about the power of literature to overcome repression, penned by
contest judge Azar Nafisi. An interview with Nafisi follows the essay.*

(MOCK NEWS REPORT)

*I put aside her roses and your words
placed them between the holy pages.
It is time to meet my warring beloveds,
you who both strive to push each other from my heart,
to mar each other's beauty,
so I may submit to one.
Shall I defer two dreams and rest,
or forever remain prisoner of a war that rages in my breast?*

(From *Reading the Qur'an in Lesbos* by Sanaa Gamil)

Reuters News Agency, May 10, 2014, Cairo, Egypt—The secret life of the
youngest Egyptian female MP, Sanaa Gamil, was revealed earlier today as she
unmasked herself as the writer responsible for the prizewinning collection of
poetry *Reading the Qur'an in Lesbos*. The book was banned in Egypt exactly a
year after its publication. Gamil's poems recount the poet's struggle to come
to terms with her sexual identity in the context of the religion in which she
was brought up and in a society hostile to homosexuality.

Gamil's revelations have sparked outrage among the Egyptian public—
and among members of her family. Soon after coming out of the closet, the

young politician resigned her seat in parliament and went into hiding, speaking to Reuters via telephone from the home of a close friend.

"I knew this would happen," said the forty-eight-year-old poet and politician. "I knew no one would accept the truth of who I am or my need to express it." She added, "But I am tired of lying, and it was time somebody did something about this situation." With her life and liberty under threat, Gamil remains defiant. "I refuse to run away despite many offers from international LGBT organizations willing to get me out of Egypt," she told Reuters. "For years, I strived to fit an image that was not my own, even running for parliament in order to placate my parents and justify remaining unmarried at my age."

Asked about her penname "Meem" (the Arabic letter "M"), Gamil explained that she used a pseudonym to hide her identity. "But," she added, "the letter also stands for '*mythliya*,' or homosexual. This integral part of my identity was reduced to a secret code—a word I dared not even mention to myself."

The announcement has made the front pages of newspapers in Egypt and across the Middle East, with most commentators declaring her "a sick deviant" who should "seek treatment." Opinion writers across Egypt called for all remaining copies of her work to be burned in the streets. A lone article in an opposition newspaper commended her for her honesty.

The publisher of *Reading the Qur'an in Lesbos* has received many phone calls accusing him of blasphemy and threatening his life. The publisher informed Egyptian state security of his situation and has allegedly gone into hiding.

Given the gravity of her situation as the first Egyptian public figure to so boldly come out of the closet, Gamil is extraordinarily optimistic—despite the fact that she is currently facing a criminal suit and possible jail time for committing such vague offenses as "violating the teachings of religion," "propagating depraved ideas," "contempt for the sacred authorities," and "moral deviance." There are calls for revoking Gamil's Egyptian citizenship. A Pakistani Islamic scholar has even issued a fatwa authorizing Muslims the world over to put an end to her "wicked" life.

John Ralston Saul, president of International PEN, is already preparing to launch a campaign to aid Gamil. "It is a terrible shame that such a talented new voice should be condemned for her honesty," he stated. Gay advocacy organizations around the world are organizing rallies and vigils at Egyptian embassies worldwide.

Laws criminalizing gay lifestyles facilitate persecution of LGBT people in Egypt. The plight of Egyptian gays and lesbians was thrust into the international spotlight in 2001, when fifty-two gay men were arrested on board a floating nightclub called the Queen Boat and charged with "habitual debauchery," "obscene behavior," and a host of other vice crimes under Article 9(c) of Law No. 10 of 1961. But never before has such a prominent public figure been targeted under these laws.

Sanaa Gamil was educated at Cairo University, graduating from the faculty of political science with the highest honors. Subsequently, she obtained a law degree from Harvard Law School in Cambridge, Massachusetts, then returned to Cairo University to teach. While working as a scholar and lecturer, she became involved with the oldest political party in Egypt, el-Wafd, eventually winning a seat in parliament. Outspoken and highly intelligent, Gamil was a force to be reckoned with and one of the party's leading lights.

El-Wafd has not issued a statement on Gamil's situation. None of her fellow MPs would agree to speak to Reuters regarding this matter. Gamil, however, has no regrets. "I am hoping by this gesture to demonstrate that those of other sexual orientations do exist, that we are not devious monsters, that we are human beings," she stated. "I hope that my action will prompt others like me to reclaim their voices and lives. For the longer we wait, the more they will take from us."

WANTED FOR INSPIRING ARAB AND IRANIAN DISSIDENTS

AN INTERVIEW WITH BESTSELLING AUTHOR AND CONTEST JUDGE AZAR NAFISI

Azar Nafisi's international bestseller *Reading Lolita in Tehran* inspired the young Egyptian essayist "H.H.," whose contribution centered around a book of poetry provocatively titled *Reading the Qur'an in Lesbos*. At the time the

following interview took place, Nafisi had just released a new memoir—
Things I've Been Silent About—that delved far deeper into her personal history, revealing long-buried family secrets while tracing Iran's modern history.
A long-serving judge for the contest, Nafisi spoke about breaking the silence,
perceptions of Middle Eastern women, and writing about the truth.

*The second sentence of the new book reveals that your
father was unfaithful to your mother. A torrent of intimate
family and personal details follows, including your own
molestation as a child. Why did you share these secrets?*
As a writer, you can't reveal the world without revealing yourself. My mother
died just as *Reading Lolita in Tehran* was being published. Her passing triggered this new book in the sense that I needed to address the family stories
that had haunted me for years. I write not as tabloid scandal, but to provoke
discussion. Things we don't talk about don't exist. I also wanted to share my
personal story in the backdrop of Iran's modern history so Americans would
stop seeing Iranians and Middle Easterners in general as exotic. My family,
my friends, and I are all human beings, with good and bad qualities. We are
not a different species or strange creatures of the imagination. People forget
that women in Iran had the right to vote decades before the women of Swit-
zerland. Finally, it is important to examine and question ourselves and our
societies. Writers should have the courage to confront reality and describe it
truthfully.

*You describe in the book how you initially
supported the 1979 revolution. Why?*
I was a naïve supporter of the Islamic Revolution. We were so excited about
the Shah's removal that we assumed whatever would replace his rule would
be better. But, instead, we enabled an even more tyrannical system. Being
frustrated with the repressive status quo is not enough. We must establish a
culture of pluralism, a democratic attitude that accepts and celebrates individuality and difference. It is vital that the young generation understand and
appreciate these values. In my generation, we took our freedom for granted as

we came of age in the 1960s and 1970s. It was my grandmother's generation that had struggled for women's independence after the 1905 constitutional revolution. Of course, my daughter's generation grew up with that independence once again removed. Now women are sometimes arrested simply for having the "wrong" hairstyle. But privacy and individuality should not be confiscated by any government. The basic rights of all individuals to define themselves as they choose must not be violated. And to achieve this goal we must break our silence.

What advice would you give to young writers struggling to write an essay for the contest, perhaps because they feel ashamed about discussing problems in their society or sharing their own dreams for a different future?

It is okay and even healthy to write on things you have been silent about. For instance, I am hopeful for change in the Middle East precisely because we are in a crisis and are questioning ourselves. For some in the Muslim world, the response to such questioning is expressed in extreme violence. But we must encourage the process of questioning—and positive responses. If you do not confront the truth, you cannot be a good writer. And the truth is not simply facts: truth is what lies behind the facts. Hold up a mirror to your society and yourself. If you are a young woman in Saudi Arabia who dreams of driving, you deserve that right and no one should take it away from you. Speaking out also helps the international community more than the dominating voices of extremists. Every fresh Bin Laden tape is headline news, but the voices of the young essay writers must also be heard. The pursuit of happiness is not a right only for people in the West. People in the Muslim world need to reclaim their rights, and young Americans need to stand in solidarity with this civil rights struggle. So write an essay that celebrates your individuality and what you can do to make positive change. You don't have to be a president or a martyr for your life to be worthy.

THE SACRED MEMBRANE

S.M.—Morocco—Age 24

While North Africa is typically described as part of the "Arab world," much of the Maghreb's populace is more accurately described as ethnically "Amazigh." This term applies to a diverse group of non-Arab peoples sometimes referred to as "Berbers"—a term considered derogatory as it derives from the word "barbarian." The Amazigh peoples lived across North Africa for centuries before Arab invaders arrived from the east. They resisted Muslim conquest for years, and while most Amazigh today are Muslim, many still retain indigenous traditions and languages. Indeed, it is possible to visit villages in Morocco where older women do not speak Arabic.

Throughout the last half century or so, the postcolonial governments of Morocco, Algeria, Libya, and Tunisia have sought to stamp out Amazigh cultures. To do so, they adopted national narratives marginalizing Amazigh identity, with new constitutions emphasizing exclusively their countries' Arab identities. Amazighs did not make it into history texts taught in school; their music and artistic heritage were kept out of state media.

Luckily, the tide started to turn with the emergence of a new generation of Amazigh activists who, to cite but one example, pushed the Moroccan government to teach one of the Amazigh languages in state schools and to introduce a state-funded channel broadcasting in the various Amazigh dialects. Similar relative progress has been seen in neighboring Algeria. Despite these small victories, rehabilitating Amazigh culture and identity remains a key challenge, as do widespread prejudices framing the Amazigh as "uncouth" or "primitive."

The author of this essay is an Amazigh who, by her own account, is leading a double life. She mirrors her repressed Amazigh identity—speaking

Arabic in public to avoid stigmatization—with her repressed sexual identity. And so the highly political opening paragraph of her essay soon gives way to a starkly intimate portrait of a young woman wrestling with her personal values and paying a steep price for lifestyle choices. Purity and shame are intertwined in a combustible mix.

The essay deserves to be read on its own terms: as the meditation of a young North African woman on the severe impact of social mores on her own life. Her prose is blunt and her plight compelling. At the same time, because the author parallels ethnicity and sexuality, the essay also invites readers to consider it a metaphor for the internal struggles faced by dissidents throughout the Middle East, regardless of their cause. The author's family can stand in for the larger society. Her life-or-death need to please them coupled with her impulsively human need to explore her individuality together provide a narrative tension that represents something larger than her own particular story.

The essay's closing lines embody these larger tensions. While gratefully unburdening herself to readers by revealing intensely personal details, the author must—for pressing reasons—simultaneously implore that she remain anonymous.

I AM AN ARAB GIRL LIVING IN AN ARAB COUNTRY—BUT REALLY the term "Arab" does not match my real identity. I am an Amazigh living in an Arab-dominated country where my native language, Tamazight, has for decades been a source of shame. As a child, I could converse in my native language only in private; in public I had to address my parents in Arabic. We masked our identity because we sensed that many fellow citizens—and our own government—saw Amazigh people as inferior and barbarous. Indeed, our history was purposely omitted from school textbooks, a political decision to suppress Amazigh identity and strengthen the monarchy.

Atop this ethnic discrimination was an equally painful second discrimination, due simply to the fact that I am female, born into a family that does not value women as independent individuals. I was not granted the same degree of freedom as my older brothers. But my parents did give me the opportunity to study at a French school, a luxury only accessible to families of means.

I cannot deny the fact that I studied in a French system of education in an "Arab" country. But here I was exposed to "European" ideas repressed by my family back home. I struggled to make sense of the contrast between the rules enforced by family and the values inculcated at school. Inside our house I decided to keep silent to avoid any confrontation with my brothers or my parents.

Even so, I came to believe strongly that women should be considered equal to men, and that a woman should be able to have a normal sex life before marriage as many men do. Reading French magazines that presented young women with free sex lives was very attractive. (I did my best to follow all the advice in those magazines to lose weight and develop an attractive body.) Because I could not share my ideas with family members, I had to wait until arriving in the cocoon of school to discuss these ideas with friends.

Eventually, I came to reject my family's and my culture's obsession with virginal purity. Virginity, I decided, should not be a criterion to distinguish between "pure" and "impure" women. And what was purity based on anyway? Is it soul purity, body purity? Could purity be tied simply to a small membrane?

At home, I would lock myself in my room and stare at my naked body. I knew that in my society I could never share this body with a man until he became my husband. I kept imagining myself in a free country where I could bring my lover to my bed without risking honor killing—death at the hands of my own relatives.

Then, unable to accept the imbalance any longer, I decided one day to break the rules and have sex. It was actually a hard, painful experience that ultimately felt like a form of rape. My lover was ten years older. I was only seventeen and naïvely asked him to have sex with me without rupturing my virginity. We met in a secret way in his home, and we did the act.

Losing my virginity threw me into a downward spiral of depression and self-loathing. I "knew" that I had become a source of shame to my family. My future was doomed. Without my parents' financial support, I would be unable to continue my studies. I imagined myself being disowned and forced into prostitution if my family threw me into the streets after discovering I was no longer pure.

I decided not to reveal my terrible secret to anyone. It was, quite literally, a matter of life and death. The men in my family would likely not hesitate a second to kill me if they discovered that I had "dishonored" them. I cried in my room every night and wished I could go back in time to change my course of action. I even began to wear the veil, cloaking my body and my shame in the vain hope of achieving some kind of redemption.

Because the sacred membrane had been ruptured, I knew that any future husband would discover the truth on our wedding night. Fearing that I would not be able to marry, I tried to overcome depression by studying hard in order to at least earn a decent salary and not depend on my family for financial support. I showed my friends the image of a pure girl yet could not share my secret with anyone—as if the vagina is the sole criterion through which one is respected or not!

My family has begun questioning why I am not eager to get married like other girls. They cannot fathom the reason: that I could not show my husband my vaginal blood. So I am now condemned to mask my past, just as my country has done to my people. My real identity and my past are veiled by me and, at the same time, by my rulers. Any public identity I enjoy is based only upon lies.

I long to live in a world that ends discrimination based on identity or gender. I pray that my children can live in such a world and that my daughter will enjoy her sexuality without limitations. Then again, I am not sure I will even be able to have a daughter, as an impure woman cannot marry, and the consequences of bearing a child outside of marriage would be even worse.

Thank you for listening to my story. Please keep it confidential.

THE CAT AT THE BORDER CROSSING

Samar al-Mazghani—Tunisia—Age 19

The author of the following piece is the only essay contestant who is, to our knowledge, also cited in the Guinness Book of World Records. *Al-Mazghani published her first story in a children's magazine when she was nine years old. In 2000, at the age of twelve, she was cited by the* Guinness Book *as the youngest published writer in the world. Two years later, Guinness hailed her as the most prolific young writer in the world.*

The mystery then is this: Why does a young Tunisian woman who has achieved such unique success remain burdened by a dream deferred? Under the recently deposed Ben Ali regime, Tunisian women enjoyed relatively greater social freedoms compared to their counterparts across the Middle East and North Africa. Gender inequity was not the law of the land to the extent that it is in, say, Saudi Arabia or Iran. Yet Tunisian women were not immune from the intellectual stagnation that characterized their decidedly unfree society and the wider Arab world. In her essay, an encounter with everyday misogyny leads to an explosion of long-repressed frustration. Al-Mazghani's words thus offer a harrowing glimpse of the political frustrations that would soon radically transform Tunisia—and light up the Middle East as never before.

GABRIEL GARCÍA MÁRQUEZ, IN HIS NOVEL *ONE HUNDRED YEARS of Solitude,* depicts one of his heroes under a chestnut tree: "When he was alone, [he] consoled himself with the dream of infinite rooms." The character dreams of getting out of bed, opening the door and going into an identical room, going from that room into another that was just the same. He continues doing this until he sees a man and touches his shoulder. Then he heads back, from one chamber to the other, reversing his route. He wakes up to find that same man in the room with him in reality.

This description made me think about the various meanings of the mysterious rooms. I wondered why dream rooms get mingled in my world, and why I cannot find myself in the real room? Why are our dreams destroyed in silence? Why do we suppress our dreams inside ourselves until they wane or until we dream that we dream?

When attempting to cross the Tunisia-Libya border in a car with my mother and brother, I felt bitterness choking my throat and spreading along my tongue. I felt sick with anger and resentment. I felt tremendous power to protest, to say "No!" The next moment, I found myself swallowing my anger and pushing it back to my internal world. It was one of those moments that we keep in denial and wish to wipe out from the records of our memory forever. . . .

The customs officer looked at my brother sitting behind the wheel, at my mother who stretched herself to give him the passports, and at my diminishing body in the back seat. He grunted: "Are you the male companion of these two women?" My brother replied, "Yes."

When I think of my and fellow Arab women's condition, I face a void. When I talk to my female friends and sense their burden of living, I desperately look for a word which stands for unshaken belief but which has become rotten in their minds. I look for the word "No."

In this Arab world, I cannot travel alone. Not because I am illiterate, ill, a criminal, or a terrorist, but because I was born a woman in a world dominated by men.

In this Arab world, a woman is deprived of her natural rights because she is a woman and deprived of her civil rights because she is a human being.

In this Arab world, words are blown in space, exaggerated with deferred dreams, and mushroom until they become mere nonsense.

In this Arab world, we are good at tying our neckties, fixing our scarves, and signing off on blank papers.

In this Arab world, we repeat our lies time and again, until we discover it is a bitter lie we have believed in.

In this Arab world, we do not express ourselves. We live on the margins of life and emit deep regret for all those concepts we never understood, such as freedom of opinion.

I bet half of Arabs go home, switch on their TVs, watch a comedy and laugh, laugh, laugh—and then cry over their hysterical laughter.

Are Arabs heading to madness?

Here we are . . . in the same place where we were left centuries ago, identical like mice, stagnant like the rigidity of men or hills, as if one woman has given birth to all of us, and breastfed us with the same lethargy. We carry our betrayed dreams, the disgrace of our perpetual humiliation, and the disease of succumbing to anything and everything, numbed by soft violence. The chains that hamper our movements became soft hands tickling us; violence practiced by governments has hypnotized us, stealing our rights while falsely assuring us that we are well.

This invisible hand stifles thinking, tricking us into believing that the illusory image is reality. This unlimited ability to fake the truth manages to intoxicate critical thinking. This force that fossilized Arab thinking is a dangerous weapon that can turn facts upside down and hide obvious contradictions. Soft violence is practiced to convince individuals of the existence of civil rights, so that even when government policy fails to uphold these rights, it succeeds in establishing them in our imagination so that we pay no attention to the flagrant contradiction between the insanity of the reality and the hallucination of the mind.

At the Tunisia-Libya border, I stood watching the sunrise in the distance. I saw a cat among the queue of waiting cars, traversing the border with confidence. She was without a male companion. I heard her purr. She seemed confident and free to purr without fear of being stopped.

Here, we envy the animals that have fulfilled their dreams. Here, we live with no dreams, or we dream with no life. We remain for years in isolation under the chestnut trees, among the perpetual rooms. And our dreams are postponed until something happens to change this reality.

WOMEN IN A MAZE

Ahmad Ghashmary—Jordan—Age 23

*Here, amidst a chorus of powerful young Middle Eastern women shar-
ing their dreams of equality, comes a young Jordanian Muslim man.
He shares a news report that challenges readers: Did the story actually
happen? Why are men not fully prosecuted for murdering female relatives over so-called honor crimes? How can a country represented to the
international community by celebrity queens (think, Noor and Rania)
be so patriarchal?*

*The story, to be clear, never happened, and Jordanian women (allowed
to serve as judges only since 1996) comprise a small percentage of the judiciary. But the author, Ahmad Ghashmary, is real—as is his passion to
stop the social and legal acceptance of men murdering female relatives for
supposedly sullying the family's honor. While his essay implicates the government for failing to protect the lives of female citizens, the author's searing
indictment imagines what real progress might look like.*

*The unlikely activist had his passion sparked by, of all things, reading
Shakespeare's* Othello. *As Ghashmary recalls, he had just finished reading
the play—where the title character, a Moor, murders his wife, Desdemona,
in a fit of false jealousy—when he learned that a young woman in a nearby
town had been murdered by her brother. Ghashmary felt compelled to in-
vestigate and discovered that the brother's homicidal rage had been sparked
by seeing his sister's photo on a friend's cellphone. As it turned out, the photo
was of a different young woman. Nonetheless, the parents of the siblings
declined to press charges.*

Watching a drama from 1603 come to life in twenty-first-century Jordan shocked Ghashmary, who could not sit idly by. A profile of the self-described "Arab Muslim male feminist" follows the essay.

(MOCK NEWS REPORT)

ON AUGUST 31, 2006, THE JORDANIAN SUPREME COURT SUS-pended Fatima Habib, thirty-five, from her position as a trial judge. The decision came two days after Habib had sentenced Saleh Radwan to death for killing his younger sister Dana Radwan, when he discovered that she had had an affair with a male friend.

"My sister dishonored the reputation of our family," answered Saleh when a journalist inquired as to his motivation for the killing. "As simple as that."

Most judicial authorities in Jordan had weighed in against the sentence and asked Judge Habib to vacate it. Some appellate judges went so far as to petition the Supreme Court to appoint a male judge who would do justice to the "dishonored man." "What did we expect from a woman presiding over the murder trial of a man accused of killing his sister?" Saleh's court-appointed attorney told the press. "Of course, Judge Habib would have stabbed my client herself if she could."

The Supreme Court's decision has been welcomed by many.

Judge Habib is widely seen as biased in favor of women. During the trial, she rejected defense counsel's reliance on the "fit of fury" theory, commonly used in "honor crime" cases even when the murder is clearly premeditated. Many Jordanian judges, not to mention average Jordanians, believe the penal code should treat such defendants less harshly in light of the circumstances giving rise to their crimes.

But is this justice? Manar Salameh, twenty-one, a friend of the deceased, said with tears: "Dana was an angel. I can't believe she was murdered. She was in love with Ayman and they were to marry after graduation. We're not savages, we're supposed to be civilized!"

Many other friends of the victim emphatically stated that Dana had not done anything wrong, and that her relationship was as pure as any other courtly love. "The story fed to her brother by envious people was distorted," claimed Ayman, who has been kept under police protection—lest the men of the "dishonored" family harm him in another fit of rage.

Judge Habib characterized the Supreme Court's reversal of her original sentence as "barbaric" and "primitive," adding that "it will take us ages to convince people here that women are human beings, that they are as wise as men if not wiser sometimes." Judge Habib insisted that she would never throw up her hands and surrender. She said that she has the qualifications necessary to be a judge—or even a prime minister—without doing any harm to the cause of justice.

"Extremists in our midst spread propaganda claiming that women's liberation is a Western plot designed to eradicate Islamic morals," she explained. "This propaganda is false, and its purpose is to confuse you and justify acts of extremism against women. Those extremists know nothing about Islam. One of the major messages of this religion is respect for women.

"I think the Supreme Court—those self-centered 'men of law'—and the society as a whole are complicit in Dana's murder."

WANTED FOR FIGHTING TO END HONOR KILLINGS

A 2007 PROFILE OF AHMAD GHASHMARY

In the deep struggle for women's equality in the Middle East, Ahmad Ghashmary sees hope in the future. The young male feminist has launched a new group LAHA ("For Her" in Arabic) to encourage grassroots activism for women's rights.

Hailing from the conservative city of Irbid, Ghashmary explains that he first became concerned about women's rights when one of his neighbors was prevented from attending university by her father. "We cannot lose half of our society," he remarks.

LAHA targets so-called honor killings, in which male family members "rid their families of shame" by killing a female relative whom they feel has "dishonored" their family. The problem, Ghashmary explains, is not simply social attitudes in some families. Courts in countries like Jordan and Syria routinely hand out lenient punishments to men who kill their female relatives. Murderers are often given only brief jail terms because judges claim to understand the motivation behind the killing.

Ghashmary, who addressed this very issue in his provocative winning essay, nonetheless believes there is hope. "People in Arab societies are beginning to be more aware of the danger and barbarity of these rituals," he says.

The role of the LAHA initiative will be to network young activists—both male and female—who want to promote grassroots reform. LAHA's core founding members come from Jordan, Syria, and Egypt, and the project hopes to attract a regional following.

"The future is in our hands," observes Ghashmary. "We need to act now."

WOMEN UNWELCOME

N. Dawood—Iraqi Living in the United Arab Emirates—Age 23

N. Dawood's essay "Women Unwelcome" documents the plight of the Middle East's many internal refugees like herself. For all their lofty talk of "Arab unity," Mideast autocrats, and particularly those from Persian Gulf states like the United Arab Emirates, are quite willing to completely disenfranchise fellow Arabs.

The truth, though, is that Arab immigrants in the Gulf are far from being the most marginalized community. That unfortunate status belongs to the millions of migrant laborers from Pakistan, India, Bangladesh, and beyond: the drivers of the Gulf's recent economic boom. These laborers often endure inhumane living and working conditions—with no protection from exploitation by business owners. The goal is to maintain an unending supply of cheap labor with virtually no rights.

To preserve these countries' national identities and the welfare privileges of native citizens, entire generations of people who have lived, worked, and contributed to these societies are deliberately denied access to citizenship. Presently, citizens of Gulf states are minorities in their own countries. For instance, the UAE's total population includes only 16 percent who are citizens. And their welfare privileges notwithstanding, even native citizens are invariably denied basic civil rights.

As Dawood's painful essay shows, regardless of one's status—native citizen, Arab refugee, or South Asian immigrant—being a woman only compounds these glaring injustices.

I WAS BORN IN BA'ATHIST IRAQ. FOR IRAQIS UNDER SADDAM, THE phrase "human rights" only elicited laughter—as though the person speaking it were telling some hilarious joke. When I was just a child, I quickly learned why this was the case. My parents divorced soon after I was born. It fell to my mother to raise me on her own—without any support from her ex-husband, my father. Relying on her smarts and impressive résumé, my mother eventually landed a job in a foreign country. She applied for visas for both of us. But our application was declined because my father, a man I had never seen, had to approve my request to travel—the same father who had never paid a single penny to help raise me.

My mother did her very best to resolve the issue through official means. She assembled all sorts of documents and other evidence proving that it was she, not my father, who had been raising me all along. The officials she met with, however, insisted that my father's signature was required for me to travel. When they contacted my father, he reacted predictably. In exchange for his signature, he demanded an exorbitant sum of money from my poor mother. When she pleaded with him that she could not raise the money, my father stuck to his guns.

To retaliate, my mother went to court to sue my father for years of unpaid child support. But the court dismissed her suit on the grounds that my father had remarried and, therefore, could not be expected to support two families. Eventually, my mother took off for a neighboring Arab country, leaving me with my grandmother. Given our family's financial straits, she could not afford to miss the opportunity offered by the new job. After six months of nonstop crying and pleading on my part, my grandmother finally managed to convince her ex-son-in-law to let me join my mother.

But immigration did not save us from our troubles. My mother was unable to secure a work permit or legal status. Nor could she work at any single job for more than three or four months. She was forced to quit each job to avoid the Work Bureau, who "hunted" Iraqis. If an Iraqi were caught working by the Bureau, she would be insulted, jailed, possibly beaten, and eventually deported back to Saddam's nightmarish Iraq. And anyone deported in this way would not be allowed to return for five years.

What is more, we had to leave the country every six months to have our temporary residence permits reissued. (Imagine what all this hiding and moving about did to my education.) Once, we were arrested as we tried to reenter the country. The authorities escorted us from the airport straight to the central prison. On our way there, the policemen subjected my mother and me to the most degrading verbal insults imaginable. I remember bursting into tears from the pain inflicted on my wrists by the handcuffs. "Tell the little bitch to cut out the yelping," an officer barked at my mother. "Or we'll chain her legs too!" When we arrived at the prison, we were searched in humiliating ways and kept there—along with common criminals—for the next forty-eight hours. Eventually, we were deported back to Iraq with the dreaded "red stamp" on our passports.

After a few months back in the old country, my mother managed to get another job and legal residence, this time in the United Arab Emirates. I was enrolled in a private school there, as public schools do not admit "aliens." I was luckier than many other immigrant children who were forced to remain illiterate because their parents lacked legal status altogether.

Being an alien in the UAE has all sorts of other downsides, too. If an alien meets and falls in love with another alien and the two decide to wed, they are barred from civil marriage under the law. If—God forbid!—an indigenous female citizen marries an alien, her children are born without the rights of citizens and are denied residency permits. And, of course, health care is completely unavailable to aliens unless they can finance it independently.

As my personal experience attests, these draconian policies have the greatest impact on mothers and on women generally. They condemn those who are already vulnerable to even greater insecurity.

THE CLOSING OF MY ANONYMOUS BLOG

M.D.—Mauritania—Age 23

Mauritania remains an enigma to many Arabs and to the wider world. Very little is known about the country's history and culture. This desert nation of 3 million stretches between Morocco and Senegal along Africa's Atlantic coast. The country's current, misleading name—meaning "Land of the Moors"—is a nineteenth-century French colonial invention. (France embarked on its colonization of the country in 1905.)

Since achieving its independence in 1960, this exclusively Muslim nation has had its share of ethnic and class struggles, resulting in an unsettled national identity. Moors dominate every aspect of life and are often seen as seeking to impose an Arab identity on Mauritania at the expense of the black African communities in the south. This conflict was exacerbated by successive military regimes and their repressive policies, culminating in the 1989 massacres and mass deportation of black African Mauritanians.

Shockingly, slavery in Mauritania persists to this day. While there is no formal slave market, people can be "inherited" as slaves—and born as such. Slaves and their descendants continue their struggle to secure equal rights and release from bondage. After years of state and societal denial—and an arduous struggle by Mauritanian democrats amidst international indifference—Mauritania finally passed a law criminalizing slavery just over four years ago. It also began repatriating Afro-Mauritanians illegally deported to neighboring Senegal and Mali.

These momentous breakthroughs took place during Mauritania's short-lived democratic transition in 2007 when the country had its first elected parliament and president. Other Arabs found tremendous inspiration in this vibrant transition when they discovered it on their Al Jazeera feeds. Embattled Egyptian oppositionists, for example, chanted "We are with you, Mauritania!"—as they were crushed by their own erstwhile dictator, Hosni Mubarak. This brief experience of national reconciliation was abruptly stopped a year later by yet another military coup.

The struggle for women's rights in Mauritania has run parallel to these broader political and developments. Rare among Mideast societies, Mauritanian family life has unique matriarchal characteristics—a residue of Amazigh custom. Women own businesses and do not require the legal permission of male guardians to travel or work. Nevertheless, as long as they remain unmarried, young women are dominated by their families, their individuality disrespected. As a result, many young women jump at any opportunity to marry. Predictably, many such marriages end in discord—accounting for Mauritania's high divorce rates. Thus, Mauritanian women, who enjoy a comparatively more independent status than other Mideast women, nevertheless face a monumental challenge: striking the right balance between individuality and material security.

Our next essayist valiantly grapples with these challenges in her own life and work. She represents a new class of highly educated women on the rise in the entire region, financially self-sufficient (in many cases serving as breadwinners for their families) and aspiring to even greater social freedoms and formal equality. Many of these young women are frustrated as they find themselves trapped between their aspirations to more liberal values and the realities of their societies. In her essay, "M.D." recounts how she started an anonymous blog exposing the plight of young women in her society and publicizing female viewpoints normally kept under wraps. Yet, despite the massive success of her short-lived blog, the essayist's efforts were ultimately in vain, as her website became the next victim of the very forces she was denouncing as a blogger: familial and social censorship.

WHEN I LEARNED ABOUT THIS ESSAY CONTEST, I SAW IT AS A golden opportunity to ring the alarm bell about the state of women in my country. I am a twenty-three-year-old Mauritanian working for an international organization here in Nouakchott. Don't worry, I will not be offering an overlong theoretical disquisition on civil rights. I will write strictly from experience. As bizarre as it might sound, it is hardest to speak from one's own life. Yet I am convinced that my experience showcases the denial of universal rights and the daily struggle of a young woman for a small piece of freedom or an ounce of rights.

When I returned home after completing my studies abroad, I saw my country in a new and, frankly, negative light. (Go ahead—blame my Francophone education and "elite" perspective all you want!) I was outraged by the horrific situations young women of my generation often found themselves stuck in.

Genital mutilation and forced marriages are everyday realities. Girls my age generally abandon their educations after finishing elementary school. Their only route to "emancipation" is early marriage! Society imposes so many obligations on these young women. It conditions them from a very young age not to think for themselves, not to feel, not even to love—because any freedom given to a woman is one too many. Sometimes, women themselves reinforce these backward norms. Take my own cousin, who made such an ugly scene when she learned I was going to study abroad as a single female.

My society glosses over gender-based social tensions and cultural maladies in urgent need of being addressed. Young women are fed up with having to hide aspects of their identities that are elsewhere considered banal. They are tired of having to hide their boyfriends and their sexual identities as women. And they want a say in their futures.

I needed a way to react and speak out—an outlet for my outrage. So, with the help of friends from the region, I started a blog—anonymously, of course—where I discussed the problems facing Mauritanian women and voiced the frustrations of North African sisters. In turning to blogging, I did not seek to revolutionize mores or overturn social conventions centuries in the making—but only to express myself and reach out to other women slowly suffocating at the dead hands of tradition.

With a critical perspective, I discussed issues like marriage, family, racism, sexuality, homosexuality, religion, and the challenges facing my generation. I spent hours in beauty salons, living rooms, student centers, and other places where women gather, just listening. In the evening, I transcribed the conversations and analyzed their opinions. To my own surprise, my readership grew to hundreds within weeks.

Unfortunately, the blog was too successful, the readership boom fatal. I received many threatening letters, and my identity was quickly revealed. Bowing to family and social pressures, I was forced to stop the blog. (Though I continue to write articles for independent newspapers under a pseudonym.)

Being forced to shutter my blog was a deep wound. What crime had I committed? All I did was repeat aloud what thousands of other women were saying to each other in hushed tones.

And where were all the rights that our government and political parties had nominally committed themselves to protecting? These rights are buried six feet underground, smothered by reactionary mindsets and resistance to inevitable change.

But the pain of losing a successful blog was only a premonition of another to come. As the French saying goes, "Calamity never comes alone." Shortly after stopping the blog, I met a man. A very ordinary occurrence in the life of a young woman, or so I thought. We came to know each other and bonded. Eventually, we fell in love. So we decided to get married. It was far from my mind that the right to choose the person with whom I wished to share my life would be anathema to my own family. To our friends and family members, it makes perfect sense that I should have no say in who I marry, that it is my father and brothers who are to pick out a socially—and tribally—suitable life partner for me.

I should add that I am not a troublesome woman. It sounds funny to have to say this, but it is true. I have always been a good student, a good daughter, a sincere friend, and a model employee. I am not perfect, sure. But why should my shortcomings make me unentitled to choose my own spouse?

You might ask me: "What is to be done? Just give up and curse your fate!" I disagree.

Despite everything, I know that one needs to fight to attain one's freedom. No fanfare or gunshots. One must wage this silent war in the quest of liberties and respect for human rights. As Voltaire said, "He who shouts his rebellion shall not be heard." I am living proof, writing this essay locked up in my room while all are asleep.

So, how to improve the situation? How to succeed in making women in my country understand that they are not as privileged as they think? How to make them understand that they do have the right to choose who they want to live with, that they may disagree with their own families, and that they can decide their destiny, not necessarily through marriage?

I already hope that women in my country understand that they can take their destiny into their own hands and that marriage is not the universal answer. I wish our conservative society would no longer subjugate women to traditions that should no longer exist. (Please do not misunderstand me. I am not anti-tradition per se. On the contrary, I respect and appreciate my country's culture, yet I reject unjust traditions.) And I pray that women will receive the education they deserve and that their opportunities will equal the opportunities for men in this country. I also hope that a woman who speaks out and argues, regardless of her opinion, will not be considered shameless or ill-mannered. This hoped-for evolution is what you might call my dream deferred.

At this moment, from the depths of my room, I tell you tonight that I will continue to support the young women of my generation through my writing. I will continue to fight for those who are marginalized simply for being born of the wrong gender. I will be happy for a lifetime if even one young woman in Mauritania reads my writings and reconsiders her life, or comes to see the denial of her basic rights as a fundamental injustice.

I might be accused of being a coward for not doing more, or for not being more open about my activism. I admit that I am protecting myself. But every evening, I go to bed with a clear conscience for having at least tried to fight with my weapons—my words—for the rights of women in Mauritania.

HIJACKING THE SCHOOL PLAY

R.S.—Yemen—Age 17

The next essay stages one of the major ongoing conflicts in Yemen and throughout the Persian Gulf region: that between overbearing male authority figures and young women's desire for social mobility and independence through education. Poorer Arabs and Iranians are eager to cut their daughters' educations short, convinced that young women are better off marrying as soon as possible rather than pursuing careers. Despite the tragic nature of this underlying reality, the essayist also shows us how outreach and advocacy can defeat patriarchal norms and put young women on different paths. Thankfully, some progress is being made as a result of the work of grassroots activists and NGOs devoted to convincing fathers not to block their daughters' schooling. But as the essayist demonstrates, for every success story in this area, there are many more failures—that is, many more women condemned to lifetimes of dependency and lost potential.

THE CURTAIN CLOSED AND THE CAST MEMBERS IN OUR HIGH school play walked back on stage to face an applauding audience. For months, my best friend, who played the protagonist, had been anxious about this very moment. Would her father, who was seated in the audience, walk away in anger over the substance of the play and her leading role in it? Would she be punished? Would this silly school play strain her relationship with her family for months to come? To her delight, my friend spotted her father in the audience, clapping enthusiastically, his eyes beaming with paternal pride. Tears of joy streamed down her face.

Months before, our school drama team had been charged with staging a play about the importance of cleanliness. I was to take the lead in writing and directing. Then we learned that the star of our play was being forced by her father to abandon her education and marry a cousin ten years her senior. She was an incredibly diligent and accomplished student, particularly when it came to physics and mathematics. Her dream was to one day become a mathematician and win a notable prize for our country. She dreamed big because she was strong-willed, determined to change Yemen for the better.

But her father's will was obviously stronger. She came from a very traditional and uneducated family that viewed marriage as far more important than education. I was distraught by the news. I had always imagined my friend coming up with a groundbreaking mathematical theory, or achieving some other important scientific feat. I encouraged her to take a stand, to try to reason with her father. I even asked to speak with her parents. Of course, they refused to hear me out. The cousins were to marry. And that was that.

Refusing to be cornered, we came up with a new idea. We would covertly change the direction of the play we were working on. It would no longer be about cleanliness or some other ridiculous, trivial topic. We would write and stage a play about women's right to education! We ended up with a very moving script about a girl who fails to fulfill her great potential as a result of a forced marriage. The material was made doubly compelling, of course, by the fact that our lead actor was going through the same awful experience in real life.

The play did its job. School officials and students loved it. And so did the parents who attended, including my friend's father. Two days later, she called to tell me that her father had been convinced that she should continue to pursue her education. I was ecstatic. I could not believe that an awkwardly acted school play had changed the course of a young woman's life. Her father still insisted that my friend get married right then. But she now had an ally in her quest for academic and professional achievement.

This was an exceptional case, however. Too many Yemeni families are convinced that ending their daughters' independent lives as soon as possible is the best path out of poverty. Shifting this mentality will take a great deal of work by activists. The Yemeni people need to be roused from their apathy. Everyone talks about opposing the oppressive government. Everyone complains about the corruption. But few do anything about it. Tackling female illiteracy and lack of access to educational opportunity is a great place to start.

HEAVEN IS BENEATH MOTHERS' FEET

Souad Adnane—Morocco—Age 23

Morocco is a land suspended between tradition and modernity, where one can find under the same roof the two extremes of conservatism and secularism. The challenge before Moroccans, however, is striking a balance between these extremes without undermining individual rights. In the words of the famed Moroccan journalist and contest judge Ahmed Benchemsi, "in Morocco, secularism and conservatism are two parallels that never meet. But when they do, may God help us all."

The tension between these forces creates internal identity clashes for many young Moroccans. Souad Adnane is no different. She begins her essay with aphorisms drawn from the Qur'an and classical Arabic literature. Yet the explosion of modern, liberal attitudes leads her to attempt to subvert and deconstruct these traditional authorities.

"HEAVEN IS BENEATH MOTHERS' FEET." THIS WAS ONE OF THE first sayings of the Prophet Muhammad we learned in primary school. Arabic literature taught us that "women are half of society" and "the mother is a school that, if built well, builds a great people."

And yet, while growing up, I was exposed to everyday behavior and attitudes that contrasted sharply with these teachings. Girls should only help their mothers at home; the world outside should be left to fathers and sons. A woman should always be subordinate to a man, first to her father or, if he is absent, to her brothers, uncles, or any other male relative—until she weds and becomes subordinate to her husband. A woman cannot travel alone, cannot live alone, cannot go out with boys, cannot do business, cannot be a leader, cannot speak loudly in the presence of men, cannot decide. Men, of course, can do all these things.

So why are girls—future mothers under whose feet lies heaven—treated to so much humiliation? How come they are subordinate to men if heaven is supposedly beneath their feet? What happens when half of society is humiliated? What happens when the school that teaches nations greatness is not well founded? What happens when this school teaches dependence, compliance, and subordination? When it shows them daily examples of weakness and submission?

Well, what happens is the widely known phenomenon referred to as the Middle East and North Africa "problem."

Humiliation is the lot of millions of women and girls in my country and across the region and is, to an extent, my own experience. I had the chance to go to school and attend university, but I was prevented from pursuing my studies abroad for the sole reason that I am a young woman. Is it my fault that I was born with breasts and a vagina? I am still a human being with a mind and a soul. I dream like my brother does, like any man does. Why, then, do I not have the right to pursue and fulfill my dreams? Is it God's will, as many have tried to convince me? No, it is not, for the simple reason that God cannot contradict himself. If my body were really meant to be an obstacle to achieving my dreams, God would not put in it such energy, would not fill it with great ambitions and enthusiasm.

If girls are not destined to learn and go to school, if they are really destined to stay home, God would not give them minds to think, would not bless them with the intelligence and desire to learn. Each creature is destined for a specific role and is equipped with what is necessary for that role. Nothing is haphazard, nothing is needless. Flowers have thorns to protect themselves, birds have beaks to feed their babies, monkeys have long tails to get from one tree to another to look for food and to flee danger. And if I—if women—have energy, intelligence, ambition, and dreams, it is all necessarily for a purpose.

When I could not travel abroad on account of my gender, I felt a great deal of anger and resentment. I could not decide my own future, for God had made me a woman. At times, I wished I had been born a man—but then I consoled myself that it is better to be the oppressed than the oppressor. Even so, I consider myself lucky because I could attend college, because I could work, because I could choose to live alone, and because I can choose to be autonomous in many aspects of my life. But my fight is not over and my dream, the dream of millions of Mideast women, has not yet come true.

Dr. Martin Luther King Jr. once had a dream. He dreamt of a society where black and white people would be treated equally, where they could live in peace without hatred or racial injustice, where the difference in their skin color would dissolve before the respect they have for each other.

Now I have a dream. I dream of a society in the Middle East and North Africa that treats men and women equally, granting them the same rights and level of respect. I dream of a society where all little girls can go to school, can play outside, can be friends with boys; where women can work, can be leaders and ministers, can choose their husbands, can decide on their own fates, can move freely without any risks, without being harassed or threatened, without being conceived of as weaker creatures. I dream of a society where no husband beats his wife or insults or humiliates her; where no husband considers his wife a mere sex and childbearing object. I dream of a society where all men understand that women are equal to them in all senses and have the same rights to think, dream, work, move, and decide freely. I dream of a society where men find no shame in helping their wives wash dishes, clean the floor, cook, and take care of the children. I dream of men who understand that a great nation cannot be built if half of it is subordinated and humiliated.

It took decades of hard work and serious activism to enable Martin Luther King's dream to come true. For my dream to come true, it needs the joined efforts of grassroots activists in the region and their allies in the West to promote women's rights and gender equity. For these efforts to bear fruit, education is the first step. Middle Eastern activists and Western organizations should work together to devise and put to work a regional education program creating the necessary conditions for girls to pursue their studies, and for illiterate women to benefit from literacy courses. Similar efforts are carried out in my country within the Education Project of USAID, ALEF [Advanced Learning and Employability for a Better Future], which builds community centers to advance literacy and social mobility among women. If such a project is expanded to cover the more isolated parts of the region, more girls and women will have the chance to reach a higher level of education, and hence be more aware of their rights. Women will, in turn, create opportunities for each other to work and be autonomous.

Beyond practical steps such the ones I outlined, changing people's ideas and attitudes is a difficult task; it is a gradual process that needs experience, patience, time, and resources—all of which must be provided for by cooperation between indigenous activists and their allies in the international community.

MY SACRED NO!

Dalia Ziada—Egypt—Age 24

The energy of our next essay leaps off the page. Its writer is a remarkable young Egyptian woman whose story is revealed in a postscript below. But first enjoy her spirited yet painful testimonial.

MANY OTHERS, MOSTLY WOMEN BUT SOME MEN, SHARE MY dream deferred. At the heart of my dreams are fundamentally feminine issues. This is because in my Arab world, there are more women than men. In my Arab world, women are as numerous as raindrops. Yet few of them make any noteworthy impact on their societies. Despite our greater numbers and despite the fact that we are equal in ability to men, we—Arab women—are treated as second-class citizens. The day will come when we will be remembered in the history books as the most aggrieved, oppressed majority of the century—or perhaps of all ages.

I am neither a "feminist" nor a malcontent "man hater." I just want to tell the story of a mother who behaves like all other mothers in my Arab world—that is, in a way that could soon lead to the collapse of our beloved nation. This mother is my own mother. I do not write these words to win the essay contest prize. If I were lucky enough to be selected a winner, my mother would never allow me to travel to receive the award. For you see, my mother is always obsessed with what "they"—other people, society—think. And they believe that a respectable girl never sleeps outside of her own house. Not for any reason.

"Even if I were traveling to attend a conference to accept an award, Mom?" I ask her with all the power of enthusiasm burning inside me. She chooses her words carefully, trying her best not to disappoint me: "We are not living alone, baby. We are governed by traditions and habits that must be respected at all times." I know what that means. It means the aforementioned enthusiasm turns into ashes after burning the whole of me.

I do not blame my mother. She is an oppressed woman who is bringing up an oppressed girl! Since the day she was born, my mother's fate has been sealed. That fate has led her to the work of teaching generations. She excels in her role as a teacher. She is an example now. Because she is an example, she must be the person who most respects traditions, and consequently, her daughter—but not her son!—must always mind the sacred habits. The costs associated with such fastidious devotion to tradition are immaterial. What is much more important is to obey Society and satisfy "their" expectations.

Who is this Society? Tell me where he is! I want to kill him. Who gave Mr. Society the right to limit my freedom? God gave me life as a free creature. He gave me abilities to use. So why does Mr. Society want me to forget all about my God-given talents? Why does he force my mother to refuse me the right to travel—or even to think? Who is Mr. Society to tell me not to get mad? To deprive me of experiencing the joy of anger? And while we are on the topic of difficult questions, why did my father have to die before he got the chance to see the ambition that he had stoked in me since my childhood eating me up day after day under the watchful eyes of these fetters chaining my hands, legs, and tongue?

I know that one day Mr. Society will invent a new fetter for minds too. I am quite sure that my mother will be the first to use the new fetter to chain my mind—and her own. The world is ever changing and everything in the world is changeable except one thing. Only one thing: the situation of women in my Arab world. Why? Because Mr. Society is proud of keeping women as weak and naïve as possible. Oh, where the hell can I find this Mr. Society to kill him and rid us all of him?

Aha! Now I understand. "Society" in Arabic is pronounced "mojtama." It is a male noun. My mother, who is a skilled Arabic teacher, cited a grammar rule to declare that the word literally means "a place of meeting," avoiding my point about the noun's gender. Hearing this for the first time, I worked up the courage to raise an objection. Oh yes, I was brave enough to say "no." She did not refute my use of the word "no." Such a strange and unexpected reaction! Anyway, thanks be to God, at last I said "NO!" plainly before my mother, my beloved Dictator. Resorting to the very tactic used by my mom, I invoked the same rule and deduced: "No, Mother, the word 'MO-jtama' sounds like the word 'MO-hammed.'" I stood my ground. "As long as you agree that the rule that you used is correct, then the word 'Mohammed' is a male "noun," and the word 'mojtama' is also a male noun."

After a few minutes of deathly silence, the Dictator woke up to her rage. "You are a trivial, insolent little child," she screamed. "Never, ever say 'NO!' to me again. The respectable girl knows how to speak to her mother!" I will not deny it: I actually felt relieved when my mother objected to my objection and said "no" to my "NO!" My mother taught me an Arabic grammar rule which holds that "a double negative is an affirmative." So when my household Dictator objected to my objection, she unwittingly proved that my opinion is true. (Okay, so maybe I am a bit of a provocateur—but you can forgive me for this!)

Every morning I cover my hair with a scarf and my body with long, baggy clothes, and I leave my mother to go to my workplace. However, her teachings accompany me all the way there. According to my beloved Dictator, when I walk in the street, I must walk with my head inclined, and my eyes must look only at the ground. This is how Mr. Society and "they" think respectable girls walk. And while in the street, if someone greets me, I must first make sure that this person is a female and not a male. If it is a woman greeting me, I may reply with a decent—that is, low-voiced—"hello." But if it is a male, I may never reply. Why? Because I am a "respectable girl" who should not salute men!

My father used to say that the inclination of one's head is a sign of weakness and defeat. However, my mother believes that when the girl—but not the boy—inclines her head, this is a sign of her "respectable" status. Thank God, I am not humpbacked yet—though I walked with my head inclined for almost eighteen straight years.

The road to my workplace is crowded all the time. Public transportation is miserable in my country. I beg my mother to buy me a car, but she refuses. She refuses not because she lacks the money, but because of the usual, unreasonable reasons. I remind her that I am twenty-four years old now and that I am, in fact, a skilled driver—but to no avail. "Baby, I know you are not a kid and that you are a good driver," she responds quickly. "But I simply cannot accept it, that my own daughter should drive a car." You see, the "respectable girl" does not drive.

What the hell is this? What is the relationship between respectability and driving? "Does it mean that if I drove the car, I would be unrespectable or impolite?" I ask. She says, "No honey, I just cannot have confidence in you as a driver because . . . well, because you are a girl." Then she laughs. She actually laughs, even though she is dead serious. Oh, the illogic of that! I smile in order not to spoil her lovely laughing.

After deep and long thinking, I realize that what my mother really means is that the "respectable girl" is the one who does not drive—does not steer or lead. The problem is not in the word "respectable," then, but in the word "girl." As long as I am a girl (i.e., unmarried) and not a woman (i.e., married) I must submit to the traditions enforced by Mr. Society and held dear by "them."

My mother thinks that everything I am deprived of now I will have when I marry. This, for example, is the reason she refused to allow me to travel to the United States to study cinema after I worked so hard to secure a scholarship. I am a virgin and an unmarried "girl," she explains in her usual infuriatingly calm tone, so I have to postpone my cinema studies until I have a man in my life. This unknown man is my prospective husband. "No 'respectable girl' dares travel alone before getting married. Stop dreaming until you have a husband." I smile, but deep inside me, I shout and scream at her: "Oh mother! You are a foolish woman, and I will not listen to your commands anymore. I will do what I want."

As she heads to her room to watch TV, I hear a defiant poem reverberating angrily within me: "Out of severe pain I shouted 'NO!' / But my voice was weak enough to go / and the 'NO!' sounded to me like a 'YES!'"

Then I recall the one time I truly insisted on my own "NO!" That was at the age of fourteen. I wanted to join a computer seminar held at our neighborhood public library. My mother refused as usual. But this time the basis of her refusal was not respectability. She had planned her own "summer seminar" for me. Her program, she thought, was much more important than my learning how to use a PC. For it dealt with the methods, tools, and techniques of housecleaning, cooking, child care, shopping, meeting guests, etc. Mother thought then—and still thinks—that these lessons are all that a proper Egyptian woman's curriculum vitae should consist of.

But I drew a line in the sand. Actually, it was my father who did it for me. "Your daughter is ambitious," he told her. "You have to thank the almighty God for that." This sentence is engraved in my mind and flows through my blood. It is my logo and my slogan. I attended the computer training program as I wanted, and I also learned all the housecleaning stuff, as my beloved Dictator wanted.

But where is my father now to rebel for me?

That is my problem. I always want to rebel through someone else. Or let's put it more clearly, I always want to rebel through some man. I am not that weak, and my father was not that strong. My father was just a man. So why do I seek his support and protection long after he is gone?

No, No, No, I do not need to rebel through some man anymore. I can do it myself. I have just said three "NO!s" and it is not difficult to say hundreds more. All I need is to see my path more clearly and learn how to rebel more effectively. Let me, and the millions of other young women in the Arab world, learn how to say "NO!" and infuriate them—respectability be damned!

Dalia Ziada indeed kept saying "NO!" after submitting this essay. First, she was invited a few months later to a training workshop for outstanding essay contest entrants. Luckily for her, it was held in Cairo. Rather than stay at the hotel with all the other participants, she had to commute from home nearly two hours across town each morning and evening. Her mother, after all, would not allow her unmarried daughter to stay out of the house alone overnight.

Inspired by a lecture at the workshop on Martin Luther King Jr.'s successful nonviolent campaign to desegregate public buses in Montgomery, Alabama, Ziada returned home that night to discover that her uncle was about to perform female genital mutilation on his daughter. As an FGM survivor herself, Ziada felt she had to spare her young cousin the trauma. So she channeled King's spirit into a marathon debate with her uncle. The next morning she arrived late for the training workshop at the hotel, apologized for her tardiness, and then explained with tears in her eyes that her uncle had just called to say he had changed his mind.

The next NO involved convincing Ziada's mother to let her attend another training workshop, this time in Jordan. After lengthy appeals from organizers, her mother relented. It was the first of many concessions, but a critical one. At the Jordan conference, Ziada was recruited to open a Cairo office for the American Islamic Congress. She agreed, and soon was responsible—as a young, single Egyptian woman—for running her own office and developing a series of innovative civil rights programs.

Despite political repression from Egyptian security forces during the office's early years, Ziada has gone from strength to strength. She published a provocative Arabic comic book on Martin Luther King, launched the groundbreaking annual Cairo Human Rights Film Festival, and started a public debate series on civic challenges. She now travels all over the world presenting her work. She has testified before the US Congress, received a prestigious blogger award from the prince of Monaco, and was profiled in TIME and cited on the front page of the New York Times.

Even though Ziada has achieved all of these successes while still only in her twenties, she remains her mother's child. She constantly challenges restrictions in the pursuit of that elusive freedom denied her by "Mr. Society."

PART III

BREAKING THROUGH

"Silmiya! Silmiya! [Peaceful! Peaceful!]"

—Syrian protestors

CONTAMINATING MINDS

Mona S.H.—Saudi Arabia—Age 19

To an outsider, the debates at the heart of our next essay may sound as though they could have taken place in a Jesuit convent during Europe's Middle Ages. Yet for Muslims in Saudi Arabia, these are lively, contemporary intellectual contests. They add up to a monumental, internal struggle that, for Western audiences, has come to be represented by theologically inspired bullets and bombs. But the same struggle goes on, in low-intensity form, in classrooms like the one described by the essayist.

In Saudi Arabia, which—to the chagrin of many Muslims—is seen as the "custodian of Islam," the ideology around which the protagonists in this debate position themselves is Wahhabism, a particularly rigid and reactionary school of Sunni jurisprudence—predating the establishment of the House of Saud—that explicitly rejects any questioning of classical doctrines. In fact, Wahhabis' stated mission is to "purify" Islamic theology by enforcing the most literal interpretation of Islamic law. Unbeknownst to non-Muslims—and still a sore point today in intra-Muslim relations—is the complete destruction by Wahhabis of centuries-old shrines in Islam's holiest sites, Mecca and Medina, beginning in the nineteenth century. By this action, the Wahhabi ideologues sought to eliminate visual markers of more inclusive traditions within Islam.

While not always in sync with Saudi royals' penchant for the finer pleasures of life, Wahhabi doctrinarians were also the creators of Saudi Arabia's infamous Vice and Virtue Authority. These twenty-first-century inquisitors have full authority to persecute and quash any "deviations" from "true" Islam by anyone—Saudi or otherwise—in the Kingdom. The Authority's mandate extends from policing the length of men's shorts to searching citizens' mobile phones for any illicit inter-gender communications. Thanks to "Riyadh's finest," in Saudi Arabia, intolerance is the law. Yet, our next essayist courageously sets out to challenge the basic precepts of her Wahhabi Islamic education—in the name of free inquiry. She offers an articulate, intuitive expression of the values of Saudi Arabia's emerging dissident movement.

IT IS A NEW DAY. I AM ON MY WAY TO MY TENTH-GRADE CLASS-room feeling bored, that "nothing is new." I say hello to my friend Hiba and then the lessons crash in on us. A few hours later, the Islamic education teacher, with whom I have a good friendship and exchange books on different intellectual topics, enters the class. The scene is set.

> *Teacher:* Today's lesson topic is "Responses to Anyone Who Allows the Exposure of a Woman's Face." Before we share our responses, let me ask: Does anyone believe in allowing women to show their faces?
> *Students* (pointing at me): "Oh, Teacher! Mona uncovers her face!"

Suddenly, I find myself under assault and in the position of the defendant. Before everyone calms down, my friend Hiba grabs me and says, "Mona, deny what they say, just for the sake of avoiding problems." I smile at her and then turn my face to the teacher, who greets me with a smirk.

> *Teacher:* Is that true, Mona?
> *Me (firmly):* Yes.

I feel that everyone in the room is angry with me because of my bravado. If they could stone me, they would not hesitate.

> *Teacher:* Mona, you are a rational person and believe in evidence. I will give you enough evidence and I am sure you will return to the right path.

Me (laughing): I will be convinced by evidence, not by force.

Teacher: Of course. As you know, a woman's body is a source of temptation—especially her face, as the Qur'an emphasizes.

Me: The Qur'anic verse is not explicit. There are different interpretations—

Teacher (interrupting): But what is most likely to be the meaning?

Me: There is no right or wrong meaning. There are differences, which is a
sign that our merciful God seeks to accommodate the entire spectrum
of mankind.

The teacher tries to expand her argument, hopelessly, as if she has never heard
of the different schools of interpretation. And, as usual, our opinions diverge
and clash.

Me: Apart from arguments, our religion has four schools from which we derive regulations and legal opinions. All the interpretations of our clerics
and scholars are correct. We have the freedom to choose from among the
schools the one that best suits us. Allowing women to show their faces is
one of the things sanctioned under the religious school to which I belong.

Teacher: But in our country, there is only one religious school, or denomina-
tion, that we should all follow.

Me: Do you mean that, in order for me to be a good citizen, you should strip
me of my religious freedom? This is illogical!

We are deadlocked. I say that difference of opinion in our world is a blessing,
that this is one of the laws of the universe, while the teacher replies by citing
the temptation of women showing their eyes and nose. She is seemingly immune to logic.

Teacher: You need to change your ideas, Mona. You have departed from the
consensus.

This is a serious charge. In one breath she has impugned both my piety and
my patriotism. Thankfully, the bell interrupts her before she can attack me

further. The class ends with an undeclared war, and it is clear that its fires are still smoldering. I look at the blackboard after the teacher leaves. I see writing on the board that reads, "Difference of opinion does not spoil friendship." The handwriting is that of my teacher.

During the break, everyone gathers around me, determined to persuade me and thus strip me of my religious freedom. At the end of the school day, as I walk past the Prayer Room, the teacher catches me and calls, "Mona, please!"

> *Teacher:* Mona, I know that you won't change your mind. My only request is that you not contaminate your friends' faith. Keep your opinions to yourself.

She then takes out of her bag all the books she had previously borrowed from me, returning them with a curt, insincere "thank you." I am shocked. I walk away with a heavy heart, dragging my feet and staring astounded at the books. I feel that the teacher has broken her promise that "difference of opinion does not spoil friendship." Indeed, a difference of opinion *has* ended our friendship.

Days pass. The teacher enters the classroom and writes "Rational Evidence of the Existence of God" on the blackboard. I look over the answers and the prepackaged evidence that is simply an exercise in tautology and unworthy of serious thought. As I drown in my silence, the teacher's voice peaks, calling my name.

> *Teacher:* Mona, cite the main points I have discussed today.
>
> *Me (my heart racing):* I want to say something . . .
>
> *Teacher (in astonishment):* Don't you believe in God, His existence, His names, His attributes? Do you even believe, Mona? Do you know of the punishments that await on Judgment Day should you reject God?
>
> *Me (hurt):* Yes, of course, I—
>
> *Teacher:* Okay, proceed.

Me (in a low voice): How can we postulate rational evidence of God's existence? How can we give the human mind the license to give us evidence and truth? How can the human mind, which is limited by space and time, provide evidence of the existence of God, the Creator of space and time? I do not deny that it can, but the issue is relative. The very limitation of one's mind is the first proof of the existence of this most awesome Creator.

Teacher (seeming blissful): God bless you! If we differed on the secondary issues, it does not mean that we differ on the pillars and sources.

I sit in my chair and sigh. At that point, my classmates turn to the teacher, seeking confirmation that what I have said is correct, as they have deemed me a pariah who cannot be trusted without the teacher's preapproval! Later on, my friend Hiba justifies the teacher's initial position by telling me while grasping my hand firmly, "Mona, we live in an age plagued with challenging internal strife endangering the *ummah* . . . especially a woman's face."

Me: My dear sister, our strife is not in a face that marinates itself in dirt five times a day while praying to God. Rather it is in the hearts and minds blinded by hostility to difference. Tell me, why do they think I am accused of being a "liberal" and impugning religion just because I have a different opinion? Why does the teacher monopolize and censor the process of Qur'anic interpretation while restricting me to one path of religious thought? Why has uni-polarity of thought and religious opinion come to be our ideal? Why do we suppress any difference? Why does the teacher question my patriotism and condemn me for my belief in religious freedom? Where is the intellectual and religious pluralism whose rhetoric we hear but whose application never materializes? How can you explain the teacher's implicitly threatening words of my severe punishment on Judgment Day, when I never disbelieved in the almighty God? Why does she think badly of me over one difference of opinion? Truth be told, sister, we are waging undeclared war against one another because of our difference of opinion and because of the freedom granted to us by religion and rite. Dear sister, the strife resides within us and within our souls, and not in our time. As the poem says:

> *We blame our age for our strife,*
> *Yet the fault lies within us,*
> *And our age has no fault but us.*
> *We criticize our time for no offense of its own,*
> *But if this time were to speak,*
> *It would damn us.*

BREAKING NEWS: EGYPTIAN APOSTATE REFUSES ASYLUM

Tarek Shahin—Egypt—Age 23

Conan O'Brien no longer hosts The Tonight Show, *and Hillary Clinton never did become president. On these two points, the following essay (written in 2006) failed to accurately predict the future. But while certain elements of the essay's mock news article are delightfully fantastic, the piece also depicts the Middle East's all-too-gritty reality, in which seemingly offhand expressions of personal opinion can become matters of life and death. As the article notes, the alleged "crime" of apostasy by Muslim-born individuals indeed carries the death penalty under strict interpretations of Islamic law.*

The backdrop to this essay is one of the most sordid "clash of civilizations" affairs in recent memory: the 2006 Danish cartoon riots that saw a global outbreak of Muslim outrage over the caricatures depicting Mohammed—including one showing the Prophet with a bomb in his turban. The West was baffled by the fury and, in some cases the violence, unleashed by the cartoons. On the Muslim side, the party line was that the West had no respect for Muslim religious sentiments.

The incident escalated rapidly, courtesy of Islamist televangelists and Arab dictators who saw an opportunity to regain some street credit by harnessing latent anti-Western sentiments and exploiting their citizens' genuine piety. This rather clever strategy culminated in a yearly demand by the Organization of the Islamic Conference that the United Nations criminalize "blasphemy" and "disrespect of religions." While such efforts have thankfully been thwarted thus far, the cartoon incident—and the cynical reaction of

Islamists and Mideast autocrats alike—had a chilling effect on public criti-
cal conversations about Islam going forward.

Media coverage of the affair obscured the fact that not all Muslims fell
for the Islamists' manipulation. In fact, amidst the uproar many Muslims
fought—in vain—to be heard. These moderate voices were concerned that
by accepting the anti-cartoon backlash as an authentic "Islamic" attitude,
the Western world risked undermining what little margin for free speech
they had left in their societies. Tarek Shahin was one of those voices. His
essay, which won the top prize in the inaugural edition of the contest back
in 2006, ended up sparking a minor sensation in its own right. That story
is related at the end.

(MOCK NEWS REPORT)

Reuters News Agency, May 10, 2012, Cairo, Egypt—The Egyptian man who publicly denounced Islam and whose life has been threatened by Islamic clerics has refused an offer of asylum granted by the United States, a representative of the United Nations Human Rights Council said on Wednesday.

US President Hillary Clinton had earlier announced that the United States would grant asylum to Omar Shukri, a twenty-eight-year-old Muslim-born editorial cartoonist, who declared his agnosticism on Egyptian state television during an interview last week.

Apostasy is punishable by death under Islamic law.

Hundreds of thousands of protestors had gathered on a main road in the Egyptian suburb of Nasr City since the cartoonist made his revelation last week, as Islamic clerics made clear calls for Muslim youth to seek out Shukri and kill him.

A representative of the United Nations Human Rights Council, which has called for Shukri's rights to free speech and freedom of religion to be respected, read a statement by Shukri to reporters outside his Cairo home, which Egyptian security forces have been guarding against protestors since Friday morning.

"I would like to extend my sincere thanks to the United States government for offering to protect my life and liberty. It is with great risk to my own life that I am turning down this asylum grant, for I do not wish to live in a world in which one must seek liberty away from home. I will have accomplished nothing. I believe in the Egyptian soul, and I will walk tall in the city of Cairo."

Shukri has not left his home since Thursday. His family could not be reached for comment but are believed to be at home with him.

A statement issued by the White House after Shukri's public refusal read: "We regret to hear that Omar Shukri has declined our grant of asylum. We assure him that the United States was built by millions of those who sought liberty away from repressive societies. We will, however, work closely with the Egyptian government to ensure Mr. Shukri's safety against any forms of terror or persecution."

The American University in Cairo (AUC) graduate, who had gained modest fame as a cartoonist with works published in some of Egypt's leading Arabic and English outlets, sparked the controversy during a regular interview on a popular teen-themed variety show on state television last Thursday.

As the interviewer discussed Shukri's latest endeavor in comic books, Shukri made an impromptu announcement that he is agnostic and did not believe in a heaven or a hell.

"You know, I was just reading about something called apostasy. A Muslim should die if he does not believe Islam is the right religion. How is that just? I was born a Muslim but when I grew up, I found the whole story hard to believe. I'm agnostic. How is that punishable by death?"

The interview immediately cut to a commercial break and was not resumed.

The announcement made the front pages of local newspapers in Egypt and across the Middle East on the day following the interview. The Egyptian interior ministry issued a statement calling for the nation's citizens to uphold its majority religion and respect its culture, but made no direct reference to Shukri or the interview. Egyptian law is a sometimes ambiguous blend of Shari'a and French civil law. Though many public figures have been accused of apostasy in the past, none have been prosecuted for the "crime" per se. Nor has anyone been executed for it.

However, in 1995, an Egyptian court ruled university professor Nasser Abou Zeid an apostate and, by virtue of the ruling, he was forced to divorce his wife under Islamic law. Abou Zeid remains in self-imposed exile in Europe. A year earlier, Egyptian Nobel Laureate Naguib Mahfouz was stabbed in the neck and severely injured by a young man who had been made to believe Mahfouz was an apostate on account of a novel he had penned.

The Saudi government issued a statement last week saying apostates should have no place in the world. Iranian President Mahmoud Ahmadinejad called for Shukri's death, echoing a similar call made decades ago by Ayatollah Khomeini regarding British writer Salman Rushdie.

British Foreign Secretary Anthony Brosnan said in a press conference that he was "sick and tired of having to endure calls for the murder of innocent civilians guilty of nothing more than asserting their universal rights." In reaction to Shukri's refusal to accept asylum, Mr. Brosnan said, "I admire this young man's bravery and his faith in his homeland, but I call for him to consider his own life and safety. There would be no shame in that. Should he insist on remaining in Cairo, I call upon the Egyptian government and people to make this a turning point in the region, and move toward honoring civil liberties."

Mohammed Khalil, twenty-four, who has been protesting in front of Shukri's house for days, said the refusal does not make him a hero. "He deserves to die. It's God's will and the will of His prophet," Khalil said.

Two other protestors, however, said they will go home, as they felt inspired by Shukri's courage. "Yesterday I called for his death," said Magda Ali, nineteen. "Today I call for his civil liberty and freedom of thought. He is just as passionate about his views as I am about Islam. We are both good people."

Nada Fawzi, a correspondent for the Associated Press and a longtime friend of Shukri's, told Reuters on the phone from Paris that she fears for Shukri's life after his decision to remain in Cairo amidst calls for his death but also emphasized that she would have done the same.

News of Shukri's determination to stay free at home has also sparked international support. Competitors in the Australian Open gathered on the tennis court before yesterday's game and repeatedly banged their tennis rackets on the ground to protest Shukri's religious persecution.

The US show *Entertainment Tonight* quoted the spokesperson for Academy Award nominee Angelina Jolie as saying the actress plans to wear a T-shirt with the words "Omar Shukri Is Free. Omar Shukri Is Home" during her scheduled Wednesday appearance on *The Tonight Show* with Conan O'Brien.

The United States grants asylum every year to thousands of political and religious asylum seekers. Shukri will be the first opting to remain in the very country whose people have made clear threats against his life and identity.

When Tarek Shahin submitted this essay in 2006, he—like the essay's protagonist, Omar Shukri—was a recent graduate of the American University in Cairo, where (again, like Omar) he drew a weekly comic strip in the student paper. He was drawn to cartoons, he explained to AUC's alumni magazine, because of their power "as a tool for political and social satire." With European cartoons sparking riots across the Middle East, Shahin was evidently inspired to imagine the impact of social and political events on home-grown artists.

The resulting essay captivated several members of the contest's inaugural judging panel. Ahmed Benchemsi, editor of Morocco's bestselling magazine TelQuel, was so moved by the essay that he had it translated into French and published in a special edition of his magazine.

The essay also inspired Shahin, who, in June 2006, launched a cartoon blog called "Cairo Freeze"—its first post a cartoon poking fun at Gamal Mubarak. Buoyed by the blog's popularity, Shahin soon went a step further and launched the comic strip "Al Khan" in the independent Daily News Egypt. *The comic centers around a journalist named Omar Shukri and his colleague Nada. In "Al Khan," Omar has returned to Cairo from an investment banking job in London to run a daily newspaper.*

"Al Khan is a story about how the lives of a group of people with very different backgrounds are affected by their being subject to the social, economic, and political pressures and attributes of Egypt," explains Shahin. The comic also occasionally looked beyond Egypt's borders. When an edition of Ahmed Benchemsi's magazine TelQuel *was destroyed on the printing press for daring to publish an opinion poll about the king of Morocco, Shahin offered a comic in solidarity—poking fun at repression in Egypt and Morocco at the same time.*

© 2009. Tarek Shahin. www.alkhancomics.com

EVERY PRAYER IS A GIFT

M.J.—Iran—Age 24

The Islamic Republic of Iran is seen as a deeply pious society. For most Westerners, "Iran" conjures images of women donning pitch-black, body-length veils and men beating their chests in mourning for martyred Shi'a saints. Readers might be surprised, then, to learn of the indignities suffered by the next essayist and her family members, not for espousing secularist views, but for simply practicing the Islamic faith.

"M.J." is a member of Iran's Sunni Arab minority. Hers is a rarely heard voice, as Iran is usually reduced to a "Shi'a nation," while her Arab neighbors are just as often reduced to "Sunni"—despite their boasting significant Shi'a minorities. By describing the discrimination faced by Iranian Sunnis, the essayist spotlights critical majority-minority tensions within Muslim countries—and within Islam itself—simmering beneath the geopolitical conflicts that usually capture headlines.

I GOT HOME FROM SCHOOL TIRED FROM ALL THE CLASSES AND from carrying the heavy schoolbag on my lank shoulders. The year was 1994.

As usual, my *chador*-clad mother greeted me and took off the schoolbag. But that day she looked sad. I didn't know why. "How was school?" she asked. "How was your teacher?"

I had been waiting to be asked this question. "Mom, today the teacher taught us how to say our prayers. Our teacher has given us a table to mark the times we say our prayers in one week. Oh, by the way, Ma, you need to buy me a *mohr.** I want to say my prayers."

Then I repeated the bit about the *mohr.* "All of my friends have one. I want a *mohr,* too, Ma."

My mother took a deep breath, then said, "Darling, we are Sunnis. We don't say our prayers with *mohr.* Every religion and tradition has its own set of rituals and practices. Some direct their prayers toward water, some toward the sun, some on *mohr,* and some, like you, just on clean ground. We all worship the same God. That's what's important."

Not much time had passed since our mother had taught my sister and me how to say our prayers. I made lots of funny mistakes while doing this, but Mother would always laugh and say, "God is very great, and most certainly He will forgive you. Because he is aware of what goes on inside your heart."

Saying our prayers was such an exciting experience for us that my sister and I would compete for who would do the ablutions first and who would get to the prayer rug first. Whoever came second pulled off the other's chador, so that she would not say her prayers first.

That day, Father did not come home. Mother said that he had gone to visit some relatives in our hometown. (I thought that perhaps he had been missing Grandmother again.)

The next day at school, everyone was talking about the prayer tables. One of my classmates mentioned that she had not done any prayers, but had filled in the table since she knew that the teacher could not find out either way. Another student had completely marked the table the very minute the teacher had passed it out to her.

I was tempted to do the same, but Mother had said, "This is a lie. To lie is a great sin. Much worse than not saying prayers. God can forgive what you

---

* A small piece of clay Shi'a Muslims place their foreheads on during prayer.

owe Him, but He will never forgive you for what you owe your teacher: the truth. Don't forget that each of your prayers is a gift from you to God." Then she added, "Right now he's waiting for your pretty gifts. Go say your prayers so that you can truly fill in your prayer table."

From that day on, I tried saying my prayers regularly. But by the end of the week, I had completed only about half the table. But Mother would not pay any attention to my entreating eyes and would not hear of marking the table on my own. Witnessing my dilemma, my mother instructed, "God has given you the opportunity to compensate for the prayers you missed. You can do the ones you missed." So I put the prayer table and my pencil beside the rug and started marking as I said one prayer after another. But eventually I got tired and dozed off on the prayer rug—the table still left incomplete.

I did not have any time in school to say additional prayers. With the completed tables due in just a few hours, my friend insisted that I fill in the table myself. But I recalled my mother's words and turned in the incomplete table.

The teacher took a look at all of the papers. "It seems, my dear daughters, you have been all very observant of your prayers," she said. "Well, all except one student, to be more exact, who got a little lazy and did not say all of her prayers. I won't disclose her name, but I want her to know that I do not like girls who do not say their prayers." Then she threw an angry look at me. "Do you *all* understand?"

I felt a lump in my throat. I wanted to cry so much. But I kept my tears for home, for my father's shoulders. But Father had still not returned. What about his job? What about his office? This was all my grandmother's fault, I thought. She didn't live with us, so my father often had to travel all the way back to his town to pay her a visit. But this trip had taken too long. And my heart was aching for him.

Our house was full of people when I got home. All of our relatives had gathered in our living room. All of them looked quiet and sad. It seemed as if they were hiding a secret from me.

"Eat your meal immediately," mother instructed. "We're going somewhere."

I was briefly happy to hear this, because during the week my father had been absent, we had not gone out even once.

Then, my cousin, who was beaming with mischief, whispered in my ear, "How does it feel to have your criminal dad behind bars?"

I stopped eating. Weeping, I went to my mother. "Tell me, Ma! Is my father a criminal?" She did not reply. I kept at it. "Is he a bad man? Is he a thief? For God's sake, say something!" I was screaming by now. "Perhaps he lied? You said yourself that lying is the greatest of sins. Is my father a liar?"

The tears in my mother's voice did not permit her to speak clearly, but I heard her say, "Not at all, sweetie. Your father is a very good man. He does not lie, or steal, or do anything bad."

"Then how come he is in prison? Are decent people put into prison?"

My mother was a taken aback with this serious question. "Yes," she said after giving the matter some thought. "Sometimes even good, innocent people are put into jail. Have I told you the story of Joseph? Well . . . they have arrested your father . . . for . . . for saying prayers . . ."

"Impossible!" I interjected. "Today our teacher scolded me for not saying my prayers, now they have arrested my father for actually saying his? I don't understand you, Ma!"

I ran away from her. I was quite startled. I did not know whether saying prayers was good or not, or whether my father was a good man or not. And what about me? What about my teacher who had told us to say our prayers? What about my mother? What about God himself who had commanded us to say prayers in the first place? Nobody would answer my questions. All I could do was cry.

At the end, it was my mother's voice that came to my rescue. "I told you, we are Sunnis and are minorities in here," she explained. "The official religion of our country is Shi'a Islam. They're the people who pray with *mohr*. Some of them do not accept us as true Muslims. The other day they closed down our only mosque in the city. We didn't have any other place to go for our Friday prayers, so we said our prayers on the lawn right in front of the closed mosque.

"They warned us not to pray on the lawn because 'we were disturbing the public peace.' But since we did not have any other place, your father and other people had to ignore the warnings and say their prayers at the same place. Then the security forces rushed in and arrested everyone there.

"Sweetie, you father is a good man, because he says his prayers and does what God commands. Now, get up and get ready to visit your father. They are transferring him to another location. We might be able to see him."

After waiting for a few hours in the police station, my aunt and I went outside to buy a few things for my father. We had barely returned when I heard my mother cry, "They have brought your father. Where are you?" I grabbed a cookie and a juice packet from my aunt's hands and ran toward a black truck where my poor father and a few others were placed behind bars. Father was crying my name. With my small hands I slipped the juice and the cookie through the bars. "I will be back soon, I promise," my father said as he caressed my hands. Then he turned his face away from me so that I would not see his tears.

My aunt hugged me and took me away. My screams filled that sad street. The truck was moving, taking my father away, and I was crying, "You damn truck! Don't take my dad! Give him back!"

From then on, every night before sleep I prayed for my father's freedom and whispered to God under the blanket, begging Him not to separate any father from his children.

During the coming days, our house was always full of guests so that we would not feel alone. "Your father wasn't very obedient from the start," my uncle joked once. "He did so many mischievous things that finally he got himself into prison."

"And you've never done any wrong?" I joked back. "Come to think of it, I don't remember seeing you say your prayers!"

From then on I vowed to myself to always say my prayers. In the school's chapel, I would stand in a corner and say my prayers. Sometimes other students teased me. They put *mohr* in front of me, or pointed at me, or whispered to each other, or walked in front of me while holding their hands across their chests (the way we Sunnis say our prayers), and they bowed.

It took a long time before they accepted me as a fellow Muslim. Using my fingers, I counted the days my father had been gone. It had been twenty-two days when, coming home from school, I saw my cousin run toward me, shouting, "Good news! Your father's been set free!"

"I told you my father was not a criminal," I reminded him before flying to our house and embracing my father.

It has been fifteen years since those days. Many times since then we have been ignored, insulted, and humiliated for being Sunni in Shi'a Iran. But we have remained, to live and to pray.

"THE LAND IS FOR ALL"

M.A.S.—Egypt—Age 25

Our next essayist's pluralist worldview was closely shaped by his father, who inspired him to treat everyone—regardless of race or creed—with decency and respect. While "religion is for God," his father taught him, "the land is for all." This was the slogan of Egypt's secular-nationalist movement during the early years of the twentieth century. That movement included a wide spectrum of Egyptians: Muslims, Copts, Jews, and members of the elite alongside the emerging middle class. But it was stunted and later hijacked by Gamal Abdel Nasser's militarist Arab nationalism.

Since then, Egypt's sectarian fault lines remained turbulent, with sporadic yet deadly tensions erupting between Muslims and Copts, one of the world's oldest Christian communities. Another key turning point came when former Egyptian strongman Anwar Sadat—in a deliberate strategy to marginalize leftist forces that had backed his predecessor, Colonel Nasser, and consolidate power—began cultivating a new narrative of a "Muslim Egypt" and bestowed on himself the title of "the Believer President." To this end, Sadat released hitherto imprisoned Islamists as a way to counterbalance the leftist elements in Egypt's universities and trade unions. But the "peacemaker" did not live to see the full consequences of his short-sighted strategy: he was assassinated by the same Islamists in 1981. Sadat's recklessness in dealing with the Islamists triggered a decade-long armed Islamist insurgency that did massive damage to interfaith relations in Egypt and across the region. The Islamist legacy in Egypt has been a massive shift toward intolerance in the values of a society with a historical tradition of pluralism.

The uprising that deposed Sadat's successor, Mubarak, initially held the promise of resurrecting that older, more tolerant Egypt. And, indeed, there were some encouraging early signs. At the height of the Egyptian revolution, for example, in perhaps the most awe-inspiring display of interfaith solidarity in a generation, protestors in Alexandria hoisted a massive flag between a mosque and, across the street, a Coptic church that had only recently been the site of an Islamist bombing. But from that moral apex, the post-Mubarak era has sadly seen the pressure cooker of Egypt's interfaith relations repeatedly boil over as a result of violent attacks on Coptic communities by Islamists.

A new low was reached in October 2011 when security forces in Cairo opened fire on Copts peacefully protesting attacks on their churches in southern Egypt. State television broadcast the assault live, with news anchors stirring up sectarian tensions and interviews with wounded soldiers calling Christians "sons of dogs." In the days following the riots, tensions again temporarily subsided, yet no one was held accountable for the breakdown. Perhaps the only silver living is that some Muslim Egyptians, horrified by the attacks, have become more vociferous in standing with their Coptic neighbors—offering a slim hope that the ideal of the "land is for all" might be upheld after all.

I NEVER EXPECTED THAT MY FATHER'S HABIT OF GREETING OUR good neighbor George every morning would one day influence the way I treat people of other faiths. Living next to George's family shaped the way I view difference. George's daughter Mariam was a teacher, and she used to tutor me. George's son Michael and I went to the same school. And while he was two years ahead of me, we became friends and, eventually, like brothers. Our two families' get-togethers during holidays were filled with mutual respect, love, and compassion.

Through much of my young life, I cared little about what was going on around me. But now that I am twenty-five, I have started to realize the essence of the tragedy of Egypt. It is the tragedy of a nation that has lost sight of the importance of its civil rights and, as a result, had to sacrifice its political, social, and the economic rights as well. I wonder what Egypt would be like if all fathers were like my father, the man who taught me that while "religion is for God, the land is for all." The one who told me that taking care of and defending young Michael at school was a good deed, indeed a duty—even if that meant standing up to boys who shared my own religious faith. It was my father who opened my eyes to the fact that a citizen is a human being and a human being is a citizen, that peace is only possible with true citizenship.

These issues came to the foreground of my thoughts after an uncomfortable incident involving another of my friends, Basem, who is of the Baha'i faith. A police officer randomly stopped us and asked for identification. After examining our IDs for a good while, he asked if we were friends.

"Yes, we are," I replied, puzzled by his line of questioning.

"Why?"

"Why not?"

"You are a Muslim and he is a Baha'i!" he yelled back. This gave me pause. I have been friends with Basem for over a year and a half, and I did not know he was Baha'i. I would never even have asked him about his religion. That is how my father raised me. After a few more questions, the officer returned our IDs and let us go.

This encounter raised many questions for me. Why am I friends with a Baha'i? Why was Basem's faith such a big deal to the officer, when it has always been a non-issue to me? Why had the officer's face changed, why was he so disturbed after learning that we are from different religions? And why had his demeanor become so rough when he discovered Basem's religion? Am I right to believe that it is not my right or that of others to question another's religious faith? How come I never brought up my Muslim faith with George, Michael, Mariam, and Basem—and they never brought up their faiths with me?

I cannot forget the day when Michael invited me to his sister's wedding at the church. As I walked into the church, I did as I do usually when I enter a place of worship: I took off my shoes. Knowing better, my siblings did not follow suit, thus singling me out. "Are you a Muslim?" the church gatekeeper asked in an unwelcoming tone. My face turned all red, and I felt my tongue was tied. I suddenly found Michael defending me against the intolerant gate-keeper and pushing me forward into the church to attend the ceremony. He sees the world the same way I do, I thought at that moment.

Our world is falling apart because our will is weak, because we lack the will to share in each other's humanity.

I cannot imagine how some view those who follow a different faith than theirs as the "enemy." I reject the notion that the first question people my age should ask when they meet someone new is "What is your religion?" I refuse to believe that my father's vision of human bonding and peace is a fairy tale.

I do not blame the time we are in. I blame the people, their mindsets, their twisted educations, and their governments. I hope to wake up one day to one soul, one heart, one nation, a nation that knows no racism, where all religions are equally respected, where East and West meet and leave the old divisions behind. My father, George and his son Michael, and Basem are all on board.

TRIUMPH OF THE HALF-NAKED

R.N.A.—Yemen—Age 25

Repressive Arab governments view non-governmental organizations as threats to their monopolies on the public sphere. To combat them, the Arab states have in recent years pioneered increasingly sophisticated strategies, including the establishment of government-organized NGOs, or "gongos," as they are called among activists. "Gongos" are civil society organizations closely tied to ruling regimes. The government vets the leadership of such organizations. Some are even staffed by government officials or headed by rulers' family members (spouses, sons, cousins, etc.). Gongos effectively coopt civil society and stifle genuine dissent.

The next essay concerns a battle of wills between Yemeni dissidents and the head of a gongo-style writers' union. The essay is remarkable for its vivid description of what the author calls Yemen's "dissident cultural scene," which includes subversive literature clubs, art galleries, and discussion groups entirely beyond the reach of an otherwise omnipresent state. Yemen's pro-democracy movement is, in major part, an outgrowth of precisely this type of "horizontal," informal organizing.

AT ONE OF THE WORKSHOPS TO DISCUSS A CRITICAL REPORT prepared by a local human rights NGO, the representative from the Ministry of Human Rights—who initially attended merely to refute the allegations in the report—was shocked to find out that most of the statistics the report relied on came straight from the Central Administration of Statistics, a government entity.

The representative, who was well known to everyone in the room, seemed smarter than most and, of course, would not have attended the events without a polite invitation from the human rights organization. He was keen on attacking the report. In a country where civil rights are virtually nonexistent, there is a sentiment shared by almost all governmental departments and officials: NGOs and human rights organizations all work for foreign agendas. The ultimate goal of these "seditionists," the government claims, is to harm the country. "Are these organizations in place to hurt national politics, or could it be that the government truly does want equal rights for all, just on its own terms?" By raising these questions, the government representative was trying his best to spin the situation in a way that would make the government look good—without giving an inch.

The government's sophistry is designed to hide a repressive reality. Security forces stop any peaceful citizen action—be it a protest or a labor strike.

As media representative for the faculty syndicate at the University of Sana'a, I had my share of brushes with government repression. Every day I scanned the long plaza spanning the distance between the university president's office and a spacious area where police cars were always parked and where new students gathered. There were always officers in different uniforms patrolling this area; on the other side there was another police car with four armed soldiers. Witnessing this scene on my way to work every day was a disconcerting experience.

I always wondered if it was safe to work in such a "minefield." Why the need for so many security forces near a university? Then, one day I noticed some women and children looking weary and poor and milling about in the adjacent space, oblivious to the security forces. They were families of former faculty members. These families had been denied financial support after the deaths of their loved ones. Did the riot police really need to be deployed to ensure that these "dangerous elements"—poor widows—would not threaten state security?

The courage of those women eventually inspired me to overcome my own fear—fear that had been deliberately created by the officers and soldiers making their heavy-handed presence felt by everyone on campus. I investigated the gathering by going among the students and jotting down some notes. I later sent these reports to as many journalists as I could and attached an invitation to "a protest." This was a bold first move.

Since then, I have gradually established myself in Yemen's dissident cultural scene. In November 2006, all of my friends attended the opening of my first art exhibition. Because I was not financially capable of putting on the exhibition in my city of Ta'z, my friends lent me money and gave me advice on how to make the exhibition a success.

The location was a first-floor apartment in an old house rented by a friend of mine. We covered the cracks in the walls with long pieces of fabric and robes. We hung over thirty paintings and played soft classical music. Two of my friends announced the opening of the gallery, and we celebrated till the early morning. The idea of the gallery came after we realized that our culture had become stagnant. Although the establishment cultural organizations no longer cared about the youth, the idea of a youth gallery was not a protest, as it appeared to some after the fact. We were interested in enriching the culture, not protesting against it.

By the second day of the exhibition, we had already received numerous notes of appreciation. One was from the head of a renowned cultural foundation inviting us to move the next exhibition to his galleries and congratulating us on our idea of putting on an independent youth exhibit.

From the exhibition an idea for a literary group was born. We called it "Al 'Arateet" which means "the half-naked." The group started meeting in restaurants and cafés. But the writers' union targeted us. We organized many protests against the head of the Ta'z branch of the union, who bullied us and violated the terms of the union charter. In retaliation, the union boss threatened us and singled us out for refusing to work for the union.

After months of wrangling with this unpleasant tyrant, we decided it would be better for us to join the union, to influence it from the inside and bring pressure to bear against the boss. Perhaps predicting our next move, the local leadership had now decided to ban us from joining the union.

We convened a meeting with the unfriendly and aggressive boss. He was completely unresponsive to our point of view. So we resumed our protest, especially when the union would not give us a straight answer regarding the status of our membership. Our persistence in the face of threats and stonewalling finally paid off. A committee was created to oversee the application process and ensure greater fairness. Twelve new writers were granted memberships. We had finally become part of Yemen's official literary family.

November 19. We headed to Ta'z to attend the tenth conference of the writers' union. We were full of hope for a change for the better. The conference was just about to conclude after two days. The governor of Ta'z showed up to brag about the fact that the president of Yemen had asked him to cut short a trip and join the writers. Other Yemeni notables showed up as well to celebrate the region's writers.

Then a secret session was held by the union boss, who proposed a new procedure designed to keep dissident writers out of the union. After getting word about the session, we staged a protest against the new bylaw, which outraged many.

The head of the union came out and, with military assistance, tried to hassle the protestors. We did not give him the chance to overpower us. Someone announced the suspension of the conference until further notice.

The next conference was held in 'Ateeqah. The national head of the union showed up, in addition to the governor, and they promised that no further violations of writers' rights would be allowed. This was no small victory.

In the end, the results were disappointing. The promise was not fulfilled wholeheartedly at the regional level, to say the least. But what made us take heart was the concession to democratic ideals by men unaccustomed to conceding anything.

As we speak, we are working hard to create an atmosphere of trust and understanding within the union and to recruit young writers and thinkers in the hope that they will build a better future for Yemen.

BREAKING THROUGH THE SHARI'A LOOPHOLE

Raghda El-Halawany—Egypt—Age 22

Islamic jurisprudence provides men with the right to divorce their wives at will; women, however, are not guaranteed the same right under Islamic law—or so we are led to think. In her mock news report, Egyptian Raghda El-Halawany proposes a clever strategy for subverting Islamic law to advance women's rights. Marriage, El-Halawany points out, is like any other contract. Therefore, the parties to the marital contract have the right to stipulate any conditions they choose prior to entering it—including a clause granting a woman the same right to "at-will" divorce guaranteed by default to her future husband. The challenge, El-Halawany argues, is requiring clerics to inform women who may not otherwise be aware of their right to stipulate the additional condition—and persuading grooms and their families to embrace it. While the loophole does not overcome the gender inequity embedded in Islamic law, solutions such as El-Halawany's represent a step forward.

(MOCK NEWS REPORT)

July 7, 2012, Cairo, Egypt—Marriage remains one of the most stable social institutions in Egypt. Today, however, the image of a *maazoun* (marriage registrar) with his emblazoned white handkerchief stating traditional vows may soon undergo profound changes that could substantially alter the meaning of matrimony.

In a startling statistic released earlier this year, the Egyptian National Center for Social and Criminological Research revealed that more than one million women in Egypt hold the right to initiate the divorce procedure (called *'sma*). The Center expects this number to increase progressively in the coming years.

According to shari'a, women have the right to include a clause in the marriage contract that ensures their legal right to equal access to divorce—traditionally seen as the husband's prerogative—without having to resort to a court of law.

"Marriage is a contract," says Sheik Mahmoud Ashour, former deputy head of al-Azhar University and member of the Islamic Research Center. "Like any other contract, the parties can stipulate conditions. Islam doesn't deny women that right as long as the husband has agreed to give it to her. It could be limited to a certain period of time or open through the whole marriage."

Nora, one of the many women who fell victim to outdated family laws, speaks in agony of the ten years of her life wasted by her husband's intransigence. She remembers her dream of a happy marriage being shattered the morning after her wedding when her husband started beating her.

"I started feeling as though heavy sacks of sand were pulling me down," she recalls. "I went through a very exhausting journey to terminate five years of misery. It forced me to insist on a woman's right to hold the right of *'sma*." Today, Nora has a bold piece of advice for other women in her situation. "Why not secure your own divorce when Islam has granted you that right?" she asks.

Two years ago, more than 4 million heartbreaking divorce stories, which always rumble in the dull smoky hallways of the courts, triggered a wide-scale campaign to help Egyptian women fortify themselves against the treachery of men.

The campaign, with "Hold it in your hand, it is your right" as its slogan, was mainly directed toward encouraging women to stipulate having the *'sma* in their marriage contracts. This saves them from have to go through the long, painful process of securing their freedom from abusive spouses.

Soha Adel, a lawyer and the head of the Egyptian Center for Women's Rights, explains that this was a campaign responding to the clear needs of women in Egyptian society. "Egypt's divorce system grants the man a unilateral and unconditional right to divorce," Adel explains. "While men do not even need to set foot in a courtroom to end a marriage, Egyptian women must resort to the slow court system to secure their financial rights in a complex process in which they are often expected to provide evidence of physical harm during marriage, often an uphill battle."

Although it is permitted, divorce is still frowned upon in Islam. However, the Egyptian Central Agency for Public Mobilization and Statistics has found that Egypt has the highest divorce rate in the Arab world with 45 percent of marriages collapsing.

January 2000 marked a significant though partial victory in the battle to reform the country's seventy-five-year-old personal status law. In that year, parliament created a no-fault divorce called *khul'*, giving Egyptian women the right to file for divorce without providing evidence of harm, as long as they agree to forfeit their right to alimony and deferred dowry.

Many women's rights advocates, however, saw *khul'* as a half-baked solution—despite the tireless efforts, over fifteen years, of prominent Egyptian lawyers, NGOs, legislators, scholars, and government officials, who advocated for the statute.

Although the application of this new law allowed women to seek a unilateral, no-questions-asked divorce, its benefits accrued mostly to independently wealthy women who could afford to forego financial support from their ex-husbands.

In the case of *'sma*, men agree beforehand to give their wives the right to initiate divorce. The agreement cannot be annulled and allows a wife to get a divorce without having to go to court or to forfeit her dowry or any other rights she has in a normal divorce.

The campaign was a result of cooperative efforts between the American National Organization for Women (NOW) and the Center for Women's

Rights in Egypt, with the purpose of bringing about equality. Since its establishment in 1966, NOW has been one of the most prominent groups fighting for women's rights in the United States.

"The campaign's message was based on archaeological evidence from ancient Egypt demonstrating that in earlier times, Egyptian women benefited from legal rights almost identical to those afforded men," NOW president Terry O'Neill explains. "There was a sharp contrast with some other ancient societies, such as Greece, where women did not have their own legal identity."

The campaign also relied on evidence from the history of Islam. Campaigners pointed to records showing that women had the 'sma during the earliest days of Islam. Sukayna, the daughter of al-Hussein, the Prophet Mohammed's grandson, had the right to initiate divorce since she was able to travel and run her own business.

American feminists, whose activism dates back to the nineteenth century, were eager to lend a hand. American women's organizations donated almost $20 million, raised from their grassroots supporters, to their Egyptian comrades.

The campaign still faces many obstacles and challenges, especially from traditionalist "men's rights" groups. Naim abu-Aaeda, who heads Si Sayed, a thousand-member-strong organization defending men's rights, is none too pleased. Abu-Aaeda believes that any man who concedes the 'sma to his wife is looked down upon in society and viewed with suspicion. "A man who hands his wife 'sma is seen as a man with hidden motives," he states. "This is why most marriages of this kind are in certain segments of society, where the husband is much younger than his rich wife or the two belong to different socioeconomic levels."

Muslim marriage registrars are now bound by law to ask brides if they want to secure the 'sma, according to registrar Osama Abdel Aal. "Many women are simply not informed of the fact that they could hold the 'sma," he explains. "Most registrars had previously refused to disclose this condition during the procedure so as not to raise tension and ruin the entire marriage."

Women are usually reluctant to demand such rights out of fear that their future husbands and in-laws might break off the engagement.

Hisham Adam, a notable Sudanese novelist and a major women's rights advocate says that the 'sma enjoys historical authenticity as seen in the time of pre-patriarchal laws. "I do not expect a patriarchal society like ours to accept this easily," she says. "But a deep scrutiny of our history will help us realize how dramatically women's status has changed over the past fifty years. What is most important now is to have women recognize their own rights and exercise them."

STUDENT LIBERATION FRONT

Farea al-Muslimi—Lebanon—Age 18

Lebanon owes its independence in 1943 to a French scheme to create a Christian enclave within the Ottoman province of Greater Syria. Lebanon itself, however, is a microcosm of the Middle East's complex and volatile ethno-sectarian patchwork: its population is divided evenly between Shi'a, Sunni, and Maronite Christian communities, with a substantial Druze minority thrown in the mix. To ensure the stability of a potentially brittle state, sectarianism was enshrined in the new constitutional order: Maronite president, Sunni prime minister, and Shi'a speaker of parliament—with the Druze, Eastern Orthodox Christians, Armenians, Jews, and other minorities floating in between. This, in turn, spawned a perverse phenomenon where each sect acted as a mini-state, with its own independent communal courts regulating civic affairs. Moreover, each sect had its own internal conflicts between feudal lords, landlords, and farmers. With sects clashing and classes within sects butting heads, the Lebanese state sat atop a rocky foundation.

In 1970, when King Hussein kicked the Palestine Liberation Organization (PLO) out of Jordan, the Palestinian factions promptly decamped to Beirut. The PLO's arrival catalyzed the outbreak of full-blown civil war in 1975, as Maronites feared the growing Sunni influx would upset the country's delicate demographic balance. (To do this day, Palestinian refugees in Lebanon remain at the bottom of the country's sectarian pyramid, banned by law from public service and over twenty professions.) Soon, the Lebanese system dissolved into warring factions, with kidnappings, hostage-takings, assassinations, bombings, and other atrocities

ravaging the country. After years of war, Israel occupied southern Leba-
non, Iran had established a forward base via the Hezbollah militia in the
Bekaa Valley, and Syria effectively dominated the country. From this point
on, Lebanon's "civil war" was more a war by proxy for international and
regional powers, where each sectarian warlord became a client of some
foreign interest.

Still, as a testament to the indomitable spirit of the Lebanese, life never
stopped, with bars, clubs, printing houses, and newspapers somehow endur-
ing the cataclysm. Of course, the war ended in 1990 on a sour note for
civil rights, as Lebanon reverted to its old system of "confessional democ-
racy" and the Ba'athist regime in Syria imposed a bitter peace as Leba-
non's overlord via the ill-fated Taif accords. But then, in 2005, something
remarkable happened. After the liberal prime minister Rafik Hariri and
twenty bodyguards were assassinated by the Syrians and their Hezbollah
allies, a grassroots "March 14" movement was born, uniting Lebanon's
Sunni, Christian, and Druze communities in demanding an end to Syrian
military occupation. More than a million Lebanese—almost a fourth of
the country's population—staged a peaceful uprising in public squares. This
Cedar Revolution—a precursor to the Arab Spring—successfully pressured
Syria to withdraw.

The victory would not last, however. A brief but devastating 2006 war
with Israel (instigated by Hezbollah) threw the country back into turmoil.
Two years later, Hezbollah, backed once again by Iran and Syria, staged
a coup against the March 14ers. Today, Lebanon is trapped by the whims
of the Iran-funded movement, which, despite being listed on the US State
Department's list of terrorist organizations, controls the ruling coalition.

Lebanon's paradox is that while it has the trappings of a vibrant
open society—with bold gay rights organizations and a progressive arts
scene—its liberal spirit is mostly skin-deep. Squeezed between sect, patri-
archy, and ideology, individuals are ultimately defined by affiliations of
birth and political forces that can be brutally repressive. Young Lebanese,
as the next essayist reveals, are not masters of their own destinies; there
is always some figurehead lording it over them. If the March 14 mo-
ment demonstrated the Lebanese people's capacity to overcome sectarian-
ism and repression, the recent Hezbollah takeover offers a reminder that
the country remains hostage to internal and external sectarian forces. The
promise and tragedy of Lebanon is its unfulfilled potential to transcend its
founding sectarian DNA to establish a genuinely liberal society based on
respecting individuality.

INDIVIDUAL RIGHTS GIVE PEOPLE FREE CHOICE AND THE POWER
to be active agents in their own lives rather than helpless puppets forced to
accept the few meager freedoms granted them by the powerful.

In my high school, there was a teacher who manipulated students by not
thoroughly explaining the lesson topics. He seemed to choose the most ob-
tuse way of teaching any subject. Thus, students failed to get high marks and
were forced to bribe the teacher for good grades. It was shameful.

One day, I decided to defend my rights as a student. I protested to the
school administration about how the teacher treated us. For speaking out, I
failed the monthly exam, even though I had studied as thoroughly as possible,
even seeking the help of other teachers to understand the subject better.

I had attempted to do well on the exam to prove to my classmates that
my complaint against the teacher would not affect my grades. Yet the poor
grade I received caused other students to fear similar consequences, so they
chose to remain silent. What happened later made them even more scared to
defend their rights: the monthly exam results revealed that I had only failed
in this particular course, not in any other.

I submitted a petition to the school administration—but the teacher got
there first. He accused me of cheating on the exam, claiming he had therefore
been forced to rescind my grade. The administration always sides with the
teacher in such cases, so they believed him and disregarded my petition.

I realized there would be a price to pay if I fought for my rights, and pay
I did! But I had to decide whether to stop or to pursue my goal to the end,
especially since my fellow students remained fearful and my teacher only
grew tougher. It was a difficult lesson, and the school year was far from over.

The struggle for individual rights requires a large group of supporters. I
attracted several teachers and students. I carefully explained my case to them
and asked for their solidarity. By winning supporters who spoke out on my
behalf, I was able to force the administration to change its stance, and I suc-
ceeded in restoring my full marks.

Encouraged, I began to follow the news, as I now considered myself
a defender of freedoms and rights, particularly freedom of expression. I

discovered that journalists who defend the rights of others are often deprived of their own right to free expression. Two journalists had recently
been kidnapped and physically assaulted because they had published articles critical of the president and high officials of the state. I followed the
developments of the case because I believed that individual rights are one
integral whole that should not be violated.

We students, I realized, mirror the larger society, its strengths and its
weaknesses. We should be its most active part and should react vigorously to
repression in order to ensure that we—not the oppressors—will ultimately
succeed. Part of this desired victory had been achieved already. By restoring
my grades in the face of intimidation, I gained the respect of my teachers and
my fellow students. This was a good result so far.

So, when I heard about the kidnapping of journalists, I created the following analogy:

Me = Kidnapped journalist
Teacher = Kidnapper
School Administration = Regime
My stolen exam grade = Confiscated newspaper
My protest against the corrupt teacher = Newspaper criticism of
    the regime

I now understood why journalists have to fight for their own rights before
defending the rights of other people. I added the Press Syndicate to my new
formula as the analog to the Student Advocacy Group I subsequently formed
at our school. Establishing and maintaining the group required a lot of outreach work, the sort of work the Press Syndicate does on behalf of our brave
journalists.

The students living in my neighborhood were courageous in their efforts to fulfill the objectives of our Student Advocacy Group. Members of the
group working inside the school faced a lot of pressure. They were targeted by
hostile opponents. In some cases, membership had to be revoked when it was

revealed that the administration was giving members preferential treatment in exams and other school activities so as to coopt them.

We also decided to make our neighborhood the home base for our outreach work and sought the help of our parents. In this way, our parents paralleled a civil society organization. The strength of our coalition gave us courage. In fact, the Student Advocacy Group and the neighborhood coalition turned into a deterrent force. The mere existence of our coalition made teachers and the school administration think twice before violating student rights. Many students still did not join us out of fear. But while no struggle is perfect, the experience we gained will help overcome setbacks in the long run.

While I have graduated from high school, the Student Advocacy Group is still in operation, and students have become more aware of the importance of defending their rights. Strengthened by their advocacy experience, graduating students now work in several new fields. The tyrannical teacher who prompted the whole campaign has been transferred to another school. The seeds of democracy blossomed into a pretty flower that will never die.

DREAMS IN A DRAWER

Qusay Hussein—Iraq—Age 25

It is perhaps impossible for Americans and others who live in open societies to imagine just how dangerous it is to speak one's mind in the world's least free region. Basic liberty and security hinge entirely on the whim of rulers. Saying what was acceptable yesterday might get one jailed, or worse, today.

Iraqis, like our next essayist, who lived through both the terror of Saddam Hussein's reign and the chaotic first few years following the US-led invasion, realized that what truly ails the region is not even necessarily the person of the autocrat (in this case Saddam), but entire political systems and cultures that do not respect the fundamental dignity of the individual.

The removal of a dictator alone does not guarantee freedom. Thus, the insurgency following the US-led invasion subjected Iraqis to a typhoon of death and destruction. Sectarian elements on all sides were dragged into a tit-for-tat war involving old animosities, unsettled accounts, and terrorism for the sake of terrorism.

While many blame the US-led coalition for the ensuing bloodbath, the real blame belongs to the very ideologies that were clashing in Iraq. Doctrinal disputes notwithstanding, the worldviews of Sunni insurgents, anti-American Shi'a militias, and Ba'athists share a common denominator: a complete disregard for the value of human life. As our next essay demonstrates, Iraq remains a deeply divided polity. Nevertheless, her citizens seem to be slowly transcending the trauma of the three wars they endured in the space of one generation. Their small steps against sectarianism and the common culture of enmity represent major breakthroughs.

I STILL REMEMBER WHEN MY UNCLE WAS TAKEN AWAY BY SAD-
dam's security forces in 1986. I was horrified by the scene of bulky, armed
thugs dragging a human being, ignoring the cries of his old father and the
screams of his aged mother. We remained in the dark about why he was
arrested—until he was released two years later with some permanent physical and mental injuries. His "crime" was telling some allegedly close friends
that the Iraq-Iran War was claiming too many lives from both countries and
should have been brought to an end.

My uncle's plight taught me not to say or even imply anything that could
be construed as criticism of the Glorious President, the Immortal Ba'ath
Party, or the Victorious Revolution. Fear haunted me like a ghost, fear that
I might slip—a fear that I noticed in the faces of everyone else I met who, I
knew, had been taught the same lesson.

My dream deferred was born in that moment of fear. My dream was to
see the day when Saddam would be ousted and the hegemony of the Ba'athists
banished, never to return, the day when I would be able to think and say what
I wanted to, not what others wanted me to.

On April 8, 2003, I thought that dream had come true. But soon after-
ward, foreign terrorists and local extremists conspired to impose the same
air of fear that their earlier Saddamist predecessors had. I wrote an article on
"Freedom in the New Iraq" but did not publish it, fearing that those criminals might have my throat slit in retaliation for my thoughts.

However, there is one fundamental difference between Saddam's Iraq and
the Iraq of today. Unlike then, I do my best to *help* the security forces capture
those criminals. I don't want to live again haunted and terrified that I might
"slip." It seems that my dream has been further deferred. And I will keep my
article in my drawer until I realize that dream, hopefully sooner than later.

"IRAN, I WILL BUILD YOU AGAIN"

H.A.—Iran—Age 22

The title of our next essay alludes to "My Country, I Will Build You Again," an iconic poem by the Persian poet Simin Behbahani. Behbehani's poem has long been associated with the dreams of an older generation hungry for national renewal and rebirth ("Once more I will rebuild [Iran] with my life / though it be beyond my means"). The 1979 Islamic Revolution shattered those dreams, and Behbahani herself has for years been prevented from leaving Iran lest she commit thought crimes abroad.

"H.A." picks up where Behbahani left off, expressing, in concrete detail, the dreams of a new generation of Iranian dissidents, who, in the aftermath of the stolen 2009 presidential elections, built one of the world's most inspiring revolutionary movements. That movement was, sadly, defeated by the regime's shameless brutality. Yet the Iranians' dream for a democratic Iran will, for the foreseeable future, remain the theocrats' worst nightmare.

I WISH TO SEE AN IRAN WHERE THERE IS FREEDOM OF SPEECH and opinion, where the leaders are truly elected by the people. An Iran where the students and scholars dare to express their opinions, where there will be no more news about repression of thought.

I wish to see an Iran where all levels of society live in economic and moral prosperity; where, instead of the protests of the working class being repressed, their grievances are resolved; where teachers and scholars, who are among the most valuable members of the society, live in safety.

I wish to see an Iran where there is freedom of religion and where all religions can coexist in peace and friendship; where no one is obliged to follow another's religion, and everyone is free to choose their own faith. Where members of all religions are free to follow their precepts.

I wish to see an Iran where our girls and women are free to choose the style of clothing they wear. Where men and women have equal civil and social rights. Where women are not subjected to limitations, harassment, and pestering by sexist men. Where the road is open for women and girls to progress and move forward in society—as prominent men are born to educated women. I hope for an Iran where women will not be forced to prostitute themselves because of financial need.

I wish to see an Iran where all individuals have an equal opportunity to acquire knowledge, where education is free and not reserved only for the wealthy.

I wish to see an Iran where Iran and Iranians have honor and dignity, where Iranians can recover their original culture and offer their culture to the world and embrace cultural exchange with other countries and benefit from the cultural contributions of other nations. I hope to see the day when we have an open cultural space, when Iranians feel proud and are honored throughout the world.

I wish to see an Iran where there is an open economic atmosphere, where all industrialists have equal rights, and where everyone is able to produce, far from gangs and bribery, and where business transactions with other countries are far from sanctions, threats, and sabotage.

And finally I wish to see an Iran in which people of all stripes and political tendencies can join hands to reconstruct our country once again, this time along the lines of liberty and justice. So that we may return to our golden age—the time of the Achaemenids and Darius the Great, who wrote the first charter of peace and freedom. We Iranians have been the pioneers of freedom, peace, and social justice. What has become of us, the leaders of justice and freedom, today? What has made our country the global center of repression, where there is no news of justice and freedom movements, and where, if anyone utters something "wrong," he is immediately silenced. What has happened to our courageous youth? Why have they been forced into addiction and other degradations?

Things must change. I wish to see an Iran where Iranians are united to eradicate corruption and addiction and destroy ignorance, to take charge of their own future and reject tyranny and oppression. It is only through unity that one can achieve these things—the greatest gifts of society. There is no other path but liberty.

The day is not far off.

UNDERMINING DECREE SIX

S. Murshid—Syria—Age 25

In 1949, Syria achieved the dubious honor of establishing the coup d'état as the primary means of political transition in the Arab world, a plague that would soon go on to consume most of its Arab League counterparts and kill democracy in much of the region for the next half century. The 1949 coup kicked off a regular trend that wracked Syria every few years until the rise of General Hafez al-Assad—who himself appropriately took power in a coup. He was part of the 1963 coup, then the 1966 coup, and finally played the leading role in his own 1970 sequel.

Assad, an air force officer from the Alawi sect, joined the Ba'ath Party at age sixteen, turning to Arab nationalism as a refuge from his debilitating minority status. The Alawis were—and are still—regarded by the Sunni majority as adherents to an obscure heretical faith. Young Assad distinguished himself in teenage back-alley fistfights against communists, Islamists, and others. As a loyal party member, he recruited a growing contingency of Ba'athists after joining the air force, conveniently exploiting the highly politicized and factionalized Syrian army in his meteoric rise to power. He would soon effectively turn the air force into his own fiefdom and then purge his Ba'ath and Alawi comrades just before they were about to do the same to him. As the Arab expression goes, "he had them for lunch before they had him for dinner."

During his reign, Assad perfected the art of dominating Syria via a cult of personality. His gaze was an inescapable feature of Syrian life, popping up everywhere from photographs at the front of every Syrian textbook to daily TV broadcasts. Whether staring down from billboards or via his internal security services, Assad made sure to grace all Syrians with his company, all day—for three decades. At the expense of ordinary Syrians, Assad transformed an anarchic patchwork of a country into a totalitarian state. For better and most certainly for worse, modern Syria is a product of his bloody legacy.

When Assad died in 2000, the Syrian constitution was hastily modified by a puppet parliament. The minimum age for the office of president had to be dropped from forty to thirty-four to enable Assad's son Bashar, a nerdy yet vicious eye doctor, to assume the presidency. Arabs thus jokingly refer to Syria as the region's first "jomulukia"—a bizarre amalgam of republic and monarchy, or a "reponarchy." While some Western observers placed their hopes for reform in the Western-educated Bashar, the autocratic state of affairs continued. In the face of great personal risk, young Syrians had nonetheless been increasingly challenging the Ba'athist police state in the period leading to March 2011, when an all-out democratic revolt broke out across the country—only to be met with a vicious crackdown that has, as of this writing, claimed the lives of over two thousand Syrians.

Our next essayist, S. Murshid, exemplifies the courage, perseverance, and activist spirit of Syrian democrats. While her piece ends on an optimistic note, we have been unable to contact Murshid since she submitted it. Nevertheless, her awakening to the realization that "human rights are bestowed on us by God, and that no one has the right to manipulate or revoke them" represents a breakthrough that no "reponarch" can contain.

ON APRIL 8, 2004, THE MEDIA CIRCULATED THE NEWS OF A PEACEful sit-in before the Syrian parliament in the Salhiya district of Damascus. A number of human rights activists who were demanding an end to the more than forty-year-old emergency status had been arrested. This was the first and most daring protest action of my generation, taking place right in front of the parliament, on Syria's National Day, March 8—the very day the Ba'athists first came to power.

The sit-in was organized by the Committee for Defending Freedom and Human Rights in Syria (CDF). Foremost among the arrested was the CDF head and spokesperson, attorney Aktham N'aisa. Dozens of other activists went to jail with him. But the government's cunning attempts to marginalize the event and deride its message were in vain. In the evening, we received the good news that the detainees had all been released.

Days of suspense went by, and we all feared the regime's revenge for the "mutiny" of CDF activists and their supporters. A few days later, the expected response came. CDF leaders were detained by shadowy security groups. The charges against them were not disclosed. A few days after that, N'aisa was summoned to a security station and disappeared. His whereabouts were unknown despite our efforts to locate him. Then, at last, the Syrian authorities declared that he would stand trial before the Supreme State Security Court in Damascus for the usual fabricated charges (demoralizing the nation, disseminating false news, joining a secretive organization, and other ready-made clichés we were long used to).

The charges against N'aisa were brought pursuant to Decree Six, which penalizes dissent with heavy sentences ranging from five years to life in prison. The stakes were high. While everybody was anxiously awaiting the trial results, a number of individuals, including attorney Anwar al-Biny and journalist Haseeba Abdul-Rahman, gathered to form a follow-up committee for the case of Aktham N'aisa. The purpose was to oppose the regime's targeting of a Syrian civil society activist by seeking public scrutiny of the trial and providing N'aisa with legal consultation.

At the outset, I was the youngest in both age and experience among the committee members, but I was full of will and motivation. I asked to be given more responsibilities, despite my own inner fears—not for myself but for the people around me—especially after the security forces began inquiring about my activities. Yet the more repressive the measures became, the more persistent I grew, because I was convinced that this was the right cause.

On the first day of trial, N'aisa was escorted to court by a large contingent of security forces and military police who blocked the avenues leading to the courthouse. We then realized N'aisa was being held in the notorious Sednaya military prison near Damascus. I watched him drag his leg, surrounded by heavily armed officers. I felt sick and disgusted at a country that treats its educated citizens in such a shameful way for daring to express themselves in public. Overcome by my sense of outrage, I waved to N'aisa—and saw many eyes gazing at me with vengeance.

As the trial went on, I stepped up my work in the CDF legal committee, whose name changed to the Follow-Up Committee for the Affairs of the Detained, Exiled, and Revoked Citizens. I was keen on attending the trial and became an almost constant presence at the proceedings. After four months of continuous work, the efforts of the committee and its supporters culminated in the release of N'aisa—thanks also to support from friends and colleagues in Syria, the Arab world, and well-known international organizations.

I realized how unjust Syria's emergency law is and how frail it becomes when confronted by those who believe in the inherent rights of all human beings, regardless of status, citizenship, or race. I committed myself to advancing the beliefs that human rights are bestowed on us by God and that no one has the right to manipulate or revoke them; that the International Declaration of Human Rights is a great asset for all peoples on Earth, including the Syrian people; that the Declaration stands above local laws; that all signatory states must abide by its provisions; that collaboration among activists is a great force against civil rights violations and can guarantee a dignified life.

I look forward to a country that has a promising future without emergency laws and without Decree Six; a country where those expressing opposing views are not arbitrarily detained. I hope for a country where the rule of law protects civil rights, including those of dissidents like me. Such a country, I am convinced, will once again commit Syrians to love of country and each other.

DRIVING TOWARD EQUALITY

S.B.Z.—Saudi Arabia—Age 19

Since its founding in 1932, Saudi Arabia has maintained a rigorous system of gender apartheid. Women are subjected to numerous restrictions derived from a particularly reactionary, puritanical version of Sunni Islam that constitutes the state religion. Saudi women may not leave their homes without male guardians, may not associate publicly with men other than their direct blood relatives, are barred from many jobs by dint of their gender, and, most notably, are forbidden to drive cars.

Against this repressive backdrop, a report from the future reveals the story behind a nonviolent campaign for women's right to drive in Saudi Arabia. The article's energetic prose almost makes the campaign seem real. When this essay was submitted however, the essayist's vision of a successful, MLK-style campaign led by women seeking the right to drive seemed highly implausible. As strong headwinds of change blew through the Arab Middle East, Saudi women in July 2011 mounted an actual campaign to defy the ban on driving that is remarkably similar to that imagined by the author here. Of course, the real-life campaign did not succeed in overturning the ban. In fact, its leaders were subjected to arrest and harassment. Yet the essayist's dream, and its subsequent, if partial, realization in the real world, is a testament to the courage and indefatigability of Saudi feminists.

(MOCK NEWS REPORT)

Riyadh, January 3, 2014

Unlike most young girls who grow up playing with Fulla or Sara dolls—Barbie-style dolls marketed to children in the Middle East—Fatima al-Abdulaziz, nineteen, used to zoom Ferrari and Lamborghini models across the carpeted floor of her Riyadh villa when she was young. As she grew older, al-Abdulaziz stopped racing the cars in her living room. Yet they continued to hold a special place in her heart. The ruby-red and canary-yellow model cars were lovingly displayed on a stand beside her bed.

When once asked why, al-Abdulaziz responded, "I know I will never be permitted to drive a car in the real world. I live out my fantasy of driving through these toys. Every night before going to bed, I look at these cars and dream of a day when I, too, will be able to drive."

Today, however, al-Abdulaziz beams as she opens the door to her family's four-door sedan, and sits—not shotgun or in the backseat as usual—but in the driver's seat. Her dream has become a reality.

Yesterday, in the culmination of a suffragette-style movement, the women of Saudi Arabia attained the right to drive cars. Spearheaded by Hala al-Amer, the movement began in early 2009 when al-Amer, then twenty-four, picked up an Arabic translation of *To Kill a Mockingbird* from a local bookstore. The famed Harper Lee novel opened her eyes to the world of the American civil rights movement and drove her to research it further. This, in turn, introduced her to personalities like Dr. Martin Luther King Jr. and W.E.B. Du Bois.

But it was when al-Amer read about Rosa Parks and how her actions spelled the beginning of the end of racial segregation in the United States that she realized that anyone, even women, can make a difference in society. The restriction of African Americans to the back of the bus reminded al-Amer all too well of the restriction of women in Saudi Arabia to the backseats of cars.

Al-Amer was fed up with hearing tales of women who had died in their homes because there was no male available at the time to transport them to a hospital emergency room. She had also far too often seen boys as young as nine or ten driving large SUVs because there was no other male in the household who could take the female members out. Even in regard to her own family, al-Amer was tired of waiting for her younger brother to come home from college, or for her father to come home from work, so that she could go to her friend's house, or so that her mother could merely buy some bread and eggs.

Al-Amer felt it was high time for change in her homeland. She realized that if women in the Kingdom were ever to attain equality with men, they would have to commit the same acts of defiance as Rosa Parks had.

At first, al-Amer was not sure how best to approach her idea of civil disobedience. She recalled how in November of 1990, forty-seven Saudi women had driven through the streets of Riyadh to protest laws prohibiting them from driving. The women were imprisoned, and their extended families were publicly chastised. As a result, a similar protest appeared to be a futile step toward female emancipation in al-Amer's eyes—at least at first.

After one particular evening of intense Facebooking and web surfing, al-Amer realized that there was a particular tool that the women of 1990 did not have. What was this secret weapon? The Internet.

With this resource, al-Amer decided to form a network of like-minded individuals. She created a blog urging women's equality and discovered that many people held views similar to hers. Within a week, her blog had more than five thousand hits.

"I expected to face a lot of opposition," al-Amer recalls. "However, almost everyone I communicated with agreed with me when I said that prohibitions against women's driving have no basis in religion. It's all cultural."

Al-Amer began to blog more and more passionately and, soon enough, she formed a virtual clandestine group with twenty other Saudi women known as "Dames Requiring Implementation of Vehicular Equality," or D.R.I.V.E. These women networked individually with other women in their respective communities, mobilizing them against driving restrictions in Saudi Arabia. Within weeks, the group grew exponentially.

By mid-2012, D.R.I.V.E. had more than one thousand members. On the eve of 2013, D.R.I.V.E. had more than five thousand members. It was rumored that nearly every household had at least one woman in the group. However, the association worked under such hushed conditions that it acquired the characteristics of a secret society.

Throughout 2013, D.R.I.V.E. worked undercover across the Kingdom to legalize women's driving. Flyers and posters demanding women's right to drive began to pop up in the malls of Riyadh, Jeddah, and Dammam. Shortly after that, they appeared in mosques and invoked religious traditions, demonstrating that women during the Prophet's time, including his wives, rode camels. "Had they been alive now, they would have driven cars!" exclaimed one flyer. They were all signed "D.R.I.V.E."

A national witch hunt was instigated to combat the root of this civil disobedience movement, but there was no way to uncover the leadership. D.R.I.V.E. included some women specializing in information technology, meaning no digital paper trail was left. The Saudi populace began rumbling about this highly contentious issue in a way never seen before. Change appeared to be close.

The pièce de résistance, however, occurred on November 6, 2013, twenty-three years to the day after the failed 1990 protest. More than 3,500 cars appeared in the streets of Riyadh and blocked the road to the airport. Similar protests took place in other major cities. All cars were driven by members of D.R.I.V.E. In other words, all cars were driven by women.

A protest on such a massive scale had never before been seen in Saudi Arabia. While some protesters, including al-Amer, were arrested, it was impossible for police to arrest all of the dissenters. As a result, for the first time in Saudi history, women led a largely successful demonstration.

To protest the imprisonment of the D.R.I.V.E. members, citizens from the entire spectrum of society—male and female, famous celebrities and average people, young and old—took to the streets. Riots erupted in the capital and other important cities.

When asked in an interview why she was protesting in the streets despite putting her entire family at risk, Reema al-Omar, forty-three, replied: "We have been hearing that the new King [Abdullah] will allow women to drive. But it's been nearly seven years now, and nothing has been done."

Mona al-Hussein, twenty-nine, another protester, said, "Women are 50 percent of the population, and one half of the population cannot suppress the other half. It's time we take matters into our own hands."

After a month of marches all across the country and a Gandhi-style hunger strike by the imprisoned D.R.I.V.E. members, even the international community began to take note. As international pressure forcing Saudi Arabia to legalize women's right to drive mounted, the government finally penned a new law enabling women to drive. The decree passed on January 2, 2014, and Hala al-Amer and the other protesters were released.

And so, yesterday marked the first day when the famed, palm-tree-lined Tahlia Street of Riyadh witnessed not only the usual young men speeding their coupes, but women, including al-Abdulaziz, revving their engines and racing forth, with black headscarves fluttering in the desert wind.

WANTED TO DRIVE IN SAUDI ARABIA

In the following 2009 interview, S.B.Z., the nineteen-year-old student who wrote the remarkable "Driving toward Equality" essay, spoke about gender apartheid in Saudi Arabia, and shared her hopes of one day driving the streets of Riyadh . . . on her own!

Why speak out in opposition to the ban against
women driving in Saudi Arabia?
All my life I have felt like a second-class citizen. Even now that I am nineteen, when I am in Saudi Arabia, I feel as if I will forever remain a "minor." Growing up, it always frustrated me that I had to wait for my father to arrive home from work just so I could leave my house or just so my mother could buy some milk or eggs. Imagine being a teenager and wanting to go out. . . . It was impossible. There is no real system of public transportation in Saudi Arabia, so the only source of mobility for millions of women are male relatives. Now, when I return to Saudi Arabia, I see young boys—no older than twelve or thirteen—driving pick-up trucks packed with women, the mothers and sisters of these young boys. It infuriates me when I read in the newspaper of women who are in need of emergency medical attention but have no male to transport them to a hospital or clinic.

*Your essay is an article from the year 2014 describing a
successful campaign for the right to drive. Do you think
the article can become a reality—and by 2014?*

I only hope that change can come by 2014. It is 2009, and while the king
has been promising reform for years now, genuine improvements in the lot of
women, even within the next three years, is not perceptible. However, I also
know from anti-colonization efforts in South Asia, as well as the American
civil rights movement, that once the flame of change is ignited, a blazing trail
of progress is not too far behind. In terms of Saudi Arabia, while the match
demanding a revolution of thought may have already been struck, it has not
yet been thrown into the pit of firewood—at least in my opinion.

*You asked to remain anonymous when
you entered the contest. Why?*

My family still lives in Saudi Arabia, and I want to continue visiting them.
My writing can jeopardize my entry into the Kingdom. Saudi Arabia does not
have a democratic government, and my writing—though completely creative
and fictional—can very easily be considered dissent and a threat to national
security. Furthermore, even if I choose never to come to Saudi Arabia, by
publishing my name, I can potentially expose my family to danger. It is hard
for Americans to understand this when their constitutional right to freedom
of speech is not continuously threatened by their government. I only hope
that Americans truly realize the value of this right!

JUST ANOTHER DAY IN 2013

M. El-Dahshan—Egypt—Age 22

In 2011, Cairo's Tahrir Square, which stood at the epicenter of the upris-
ing that toppled Hosni Mubarak, captured the Western imagination. The
next essay was written at a time when the Mubarak regime seemed like a
permanent fixture to outside observers—and to many Egyptians themselves.

M. El-Dahshan, however, doggedly refused to accept the stagnant, un-
free status quo that seemed so "natural" to others. So he presciently imagined
himself stuck in a traffic jam in Tahrir Square in an Egypt where free ex-
pression, government accountability, and economic liberty are the order of
the day. An amusing tour of this future Egypt illustrates the tangible impacts
of liberalization. El-Dahshan browses a newspaper exposé of government
corruption, passes by a peaceful student rally actually protected by police
officers, and humorously boasts about the cheaper goods available thanks to
a free market.

In 2011, the cynics were proved wrong, while El-Dahshan's dreams
were vindicated by millions of Egyptians seeking a brighter future. Still, as
the essay's thoughtful closing demonstrates, El-Dahshan would be the last
to call the work of Egyptian democrats finished. Reaching the Egypt he de-
scribes "will take a lot of effort," he concedes. "Change will come from citi-
zen action pushing for reform and establishing freedom and civil rights as
a way of life." The fall of Mubarak has brought Egypt a few steps closer to
this stage. Egyptian liberals face numerous challenges and formidable foes—
including Islamists determined to impose their own nightmare-visions on
Egyptian society. Still, El-Dahshan clearly seems up to the task. The question

remains: will the West continue to dismiss Mideast democrats as before—or
embrace them as they roll up their sleeves to build their dreams?

AS I DRINK MY MORNING COFFEE, I NOTICE I AM RUNNING A LIT-
tle late. I burn my tongue swallowing the hot beverage, and at my feeble
expression of agony, my wife (yes, we got married last year!) laughs at
me—"Again?"

I'm late for work, so I guess I will have to take my car. The bus takes too
long in the morning traffic. I bought this car a little while ago, now that the
General Agreement on Tariffs and Trade's provisions are finally applied and
the government no longer uses every protectionist gimmick in the book to
avoid liberalizing trade. Free trade and competition are by default beneficial
to consumers, freeing us from the despotic monopoly of state-owned enter-
prises overcharging for goods and services of mediocre quality. I can even see
the benefit in my phone bill and in my grocery budget, but less in my wife's
still-pricey Italian shoes!

Economic freedom is a blessing. Heavy-handed government intervention is a real mistake. It only leads to inefficiencies that are never offset by
any gains that the treasury might acquire in tax revenues. But economic
freedom is not a panacea, and its effects may be aborted by the absence of
political freedom and in the absence of institutional reforms. It is therefore
up to us, as informed citizens, to monitor the government's activities and
ensure that it abides by the international regulations and agreements it has
signed. We must hold the government accountable for undertaking the reforms it has promised.

I stop to buy some newspapers. Did I mention that freedom of the press
is now a constitutional right? We are now free to establish newspapers and
to express our opinions, and even the most outspoken voices are now free to
express themselves. And just as we expected, the citizens are fully capable of
making perfect selections, discarding the more extreme voices—the govern-

ment's favorite excuse for muzzling dissidents!—and giving their attention only to the mainstream political voices shaping public debate about the big issues facing our country.

We have achieved partial political freedom, too. Party creation is no longer regulated by the government. It's about time, since all requests for forming political parties had been rejected in the past two decades. It is not yet what we wish for. Political transition still seems like a dream, but the dream is getting closer to reality every day.

My car gets stuck in a traffic jam near Tahrir Square. There is a demonstration organized by students of the National University. I smile at the sight of the students walking in order and silence under the protection of police officers who help regulate the traffic. A little bruise on my left shoulder, left by a blind blow from an ignorant soldier, reminds me of the times we marched to protest the government's nonchalance toward the lives of its citizens. We spoke out after a series of man-made disasters revealed that the carelessness of the authorities was only surpassed by their incompetence in crisis management.

Was it so long ago? No, it was not. Just a few years were enough for us to effect such a change. The government is now held accountable for its actions. What a change! But it is just the beginning.

I take advantage of the traffic jam to start browsing the newspapers I bought. There is an interesting article about the former minister of housing. After a journalistic scoop revealed the minister's corruption, the chief prosecutor indicted him. He is now in jail, convicted of massive fraud. I cannot say I feel sorry for him! We had wished for that to happen for a long time, but the man had always been a protégé of "higher powers" and was therefore untouchable. But he was successfully brought to trial a few months ago. Isn't it ironic that the man who embezzled funds allocated to the construction of low-income housing—construction that, needless to say, never took place— now lives in a 24-square-meter cell! There is justice in this world after all. It just took us a while to realize that justice does not fall from the sky, that it stems from the heart of society, and that those who do not seek justice will not obtain it. We learned that, among many other lessons, the hard way.

I quickly flip the pages to the column written by my friend Ingy. Ingy is a fantastic journalist, fearless and bold, caustic and critical, yet always honest. She now writes for a newspaper that she helped establish four years ago— 2012 was a great year for the press! She is in charge of the local politics section and writes a daily column in which she exposes the government's misbehavior. Today's article criticizes the prime minister, who is suspected of illegally awarding a number of contracts to a foreign company after having received large kickbacks. She calls for greater transparency in bidding for government contracts. I fully agree with her: the process needs to be overseen by the parliament and, if the need arises, by an independent court of auditors.

Is it not obvious that governments must be monitored? Well, for a long time, it was not that obvious here. And the day we realized that, we were incapable of implementing or even formulating such a request. But today, we have taken giant steps toward achieving full monitoring of government activities.

Not long ago, Ingy received threats for criticizing the minister of the interior. Thankfully, nothing resulted from those threats but the situation proved that there is still much to be done in order to ensure our civil rights.

I finally reach my office. This traffic is crazy! We should do something about that. Unfortunately, the government's policies have done nothing to encourage the urban population to move to the suburbs and towns surrounding the metropolis: there is an immense concentration of power and government services within the city but a lack of infrastructure in those small towns that have burgeoned in the desert.

A critical level of decentralization needs to be achieved before we can attempt to convince people to relocate their lives to other towns: transport infrastructure needs to be put in place to ensure their freedom of movement, and services such as schools and hospitals need to be provided in these new suburbs.

The government has traditionally been wary of going down the decentralization road because a less centralized power entails the emergence of other political actors: local representatives, governors, a whole new class of active and accountable politicians who will claim real power from the center in order to answer the demands of their constituencies.

Effecting this change is one of my responsibilities at work. I can read stark disbelief in your eyes. Yes, I work for the government now. Does it sound odd, for someone so skeptical of government?

When I first came home from the United States, I had big, big dreams—and I wanted to see them all happen at once. But life has taught me that this is not the way things work, and that everything comes to those who wait. Change does not occur suddenly; rather, it is by diligent work and continuous effort that every dream can turn into a reality. Dreams do come true. Mountains can move. No matter how long one has to wait, with perseverance, a strong will, and dedicated work, we can move this mountain. But the task is not easy. And there will be times when, with the dream seeming farther and farther away, we will want to give up, to keep the dream tucked away in our imagination, times when we lack the courage to make the dream materialize.

It is difficult to motivate myself on days when I will feel that I am swimming against the current, that my efforts are feeble and meaningless. But then I recall that my work is helping free my country and my fellow citizens. And this is what keeps me going every day. It is what gets me out of bed every morning.

It is often from the inside that one can have the biggest impact. I know this now. A drastic, overnight change can trigger unexpected reactions and can backfire with the worse results. Many things have changed in my country over the last few years. Women have claimed and obtained a larger role in society, though it is still less than the equitable share that should accrue to them.

Our minister of foreign affairs is a woman I greatly admire and trust to put our foreign policy back on track. Interestingly enough, our foreign policy is becoming more consistent. We have achieved a considerable rapprochement with our principal allies and are now consolidating our regional relationships with our neighbors, including those we have shunned for so long. Real political and economic advantages are finally pushing aside the archaic ideologies. We are regaining our natural leadership position in the region, which had been tarnished by the foolish actions of the old governments.

Things are changing slowly, but surely. I have matured, and so has my country. We are both ready for change. I never gave up my dreams. Instead, I decided to rise to their level, so close that I can reach out and touch them, pick them like ripe fruits. I know that someday soon, I will. It will take a lot of effort. It will take people like my friend Ingy, people like those students marching to protest the government's actions and, I hope, people like myself. Change will come from citizen action pushing for reform and establishing freedom and civil rights as a way of life.

It's just another day in my town in 2013.

ANONYMOUS NO MORE

Mariam Bazeed—Egypt—Age 24

Mariam Bazeed contributed the anthology's opening essay ("I Am Not Ayman!"), describing the anguish of a closeted Egyptian gay man ultimately forced to "turn himself off." For years, Bazeed submitted her essays anonymously, fearing the legal and social repercussions associated with airing dissenting views. Like her gay protagonist, Bazeed knew that jail and worse awaited those who chose to live and think differently under Mubarak's police state.

But when submitting "Anonymous No More" three years later, Bazeed finally broke the fear barrier. Her decision to do so, she explains, was driven by the liberating nature of writing itself. She had become addicted to speaking her mind—a feeling shared by writers and artists around the world, but especially meaningful in the world's least free region. For Mideast "dictators know that it is not our propensity for violence that is to be feared," she writes, "but our non-silence, our non-apathy, our non-reactivity."

Bazeed thus presciently describes the mindset that, just a few months later, would lead millions of her compatriots to stage a vibrant, nonviolent revolt that finally toppled the corrupt autocrat who for years had kept her silent. Egypt—like Bazeed—would no longer be silenced.

THIS WILL BE MY FOURTH SUBMISSION TO THIS ESSAY CONTEST in as many years. There is a world of difference between my first submission in 2005 and my subsequent ones; I wrote back then of a private theft of the ability to express oneself, of living in a culture, any culture, that is badly equipped to deal with views far from the mainstream.

Since then, my myopic view has expanded to include much more than personal restrictions—I have written about the plight of homosexuals in Egypt today, about the public inability to speak in the many dictatorships that make up the Middle East, about religious freedom, and about the rights of which we are robbed as citizens of ostensibly free states that promise us much in their constitutions and deliver very little of what was promised. I have also since expanded the venues of my writing, seeing telling examples of the power of everyday bloggers and others to reach a wide audience, to disseminate a truth ignored, unknown, or untold. These same bloggers have the power to reach the even more important audience within the Middle East itself—likeminded others who need to see that legions of discontented freethinkers like themselves exist; that they are not alone; and that they have support in their desire to change the status quo.

This expansion in my sphere of concern (for lack of a better word) was organic, natural—how could I begin to care and write about issues of personal freedom within my own culture without realizing how those ultimately resulted from much larger institutional pathologies that stifled entire populations? How could I notice my unwillingness to take credit for my writings, being published instead as "anonymous" or as a pair of initials that could be anyone at all, without thinking of those braver than I who were suffering the consequences of their boldness?

I now write as myself.

I do not think that these changes within me came about coincidentally while I was writing, a concurrence of chance and nothing else. Rather, I believe they came about because of it, because I was writing and had ceased to be silent.

Before 2005, this was an issue I had never addressed outside the safe space of my own mind. I realize now that it is this very process of snowballing that dictators are so fearful of, and therefore so ruthless toward, and so meticulous about squashing. This propensity to speak, to write, to unload the contents of our own minds is an addiction—it grows and becomes bottomless, parched in its search for truth, and more hungry the more we cater to it. It consumes us so that our prior silences of apathy or impotence seem like unimaginable torture, like a crime so vile against our authenticity that we pale in considering our misdeeds, like murderers newly endowed with a conscience. How miserably we have failed ourselves!

Our dictators know that individual silence is predicated solely upon the silence of all, and that to breach one silence is therefore to breach them all, to breach silence as a principal and unfortunate reality of our daily lives—that a cacophony of power is what is to be feared.

These dictators know that it is not our propensity for violence that is to be feared, but our non-silence, our non-apathy, our non-reactivity. My dream, no longer deferred, is for a few in the Middle East to realize that all silence is but a prelude to speech. I hear our voices now.

Please consider this, amongst other things, to be a formal request to have my name added to all previous submissions.

WANTED TO STOP BEING ANONYMOUS

Mariam Bazeed—for several years that name could not be mentioned publicly. The young Egyptian turned in provocative submissions to the essay contest, yet she checked the box requesting anonymity. But in her final submission, Mariam has declared her readiness to go public and has requested that all her previous entries now be revised to include her real name. In the following interview from 2010, she spoke about her transformation.

Why did you start writing about injustice?
At age sixteen I traveled to the United States and saw *The Satanic Verses* on display in a bookstore. I still remember the delicious thrill of picking it up and purchasing it. The book had been banned in many Muslim countries, and I felt I was being let in on a secret. That was my first real exposure to writers who had been silenced, and Salman Rushdie was an auspicious start! It seemed monstrous that his remarkable voice had been exiled permanently

from the Arab world and its unfortunate readers. Reading Nawal El-Saadawi felt the same. I decided that if they were so greatly feared, then they must wield great power. But the first time that I in fact wrote about any injustices was for the essay contest.

Why did you originally write anonymously—
what were you afraid of?
I was afraid of everything! My imagination knew no bounds, and my government had given it reason to expect the very worst. We have imprisoned citizens for the most minor of perceived insults to the system—both the governmental and the religious system. I was also afraid of a cultural backlash in a society that values conformity and vilifies those who step too far from our established mores. That is an added pressure the Arab world exerts against nonconformists: there is a formal punishment, meted out by the government, and there is an informal one, based on social rejection.

What caused you to change your mind about being anonymous?
I attended a conference in Europe on democracy and met Saad Eddin Ibrahim, who has himself been imprisoned for speaking against the government. He told a story about trying to organize a protest during an election period. Out of the many who had initially committed to participating, people kept dropping out until only 8 percent of those who had originally committed actually attended the rally. He called this 8 percent the "Egyptian bravery coefficient." If we all choose anonymity and decide not to show up, nothing changes. I am no political activist, but I resolved to put whatever talents I do have toward changing reality to fit better with my ideals. Also, would-be young reformers need to know that like-minded people exist and have a voice. After all, what initially gave me strength was discovering in others an example I wanted to follow. It helps conquer fears of social rejection, by showing people there is a community in which their opinions and their right to express them are valued.

CONCLUSION

OUR DREAM DEFERRED

ENLISTING YOU IN THE MIDEAST CIVIL RIGHTS ALLIANCE

SYRIAN DISSIDENT AMMAR ABDULHAMID SPARKED THE DREAM Deferred Essay Contest back in 2005 with a simple yet profound idea: young Middle Easterners needed to be rewarded for liberal thinking. Millions of dollars were already flowing across the region to encourage religious radicalism or buy allegiance to dictators. But what incentive, Abdulhamid asked, was there to openly express liberal ideas?

For most young thinkers stranded in the Mideast civil rights desert, the choice was clear. Sticking your neck out for individual rights carried certain dangers and few rewards. The risks: ostracism from your peers, scrutiny from security forces, and perhaps an extended stint in a prison with top-quality torture facilities. The reward: the moral clarity of speaking truth to power. Given that calculus, it is no surprise that most young dissidents would choose to stay in the closet. (Recall the title of the anthology's opening essay, a young Egyptian's feverish disavowal of his own identity: "I Am Not Ayman!")

Such silence and denial were further compounded by the outside world's general disinterest in seeking out liberal voices in the region. As outsiders offered few external incentives to counter internal forces of repression and extremism, the Middle East long appeared to suffer from a dearth of young dissidents. The angry young men comprising the "Arab street"—mobilized at regime-sanctioned rallies—seemed authentic. The few alternative voices that managed to filter out were often dismissed as freak outliers. A vicious cycle thus reinforced an illusion.

Back in 2005, per conventional wisdom, launching an essay contest on civil rights in the Middle East with a few thousand dollars in prizes seemed an exercise in folly. Yes, the contest cast a support line into repressive societies by offering a new bargain for young thinkers—share your dream yet feel free to maintain your anonymity—but did so without knowing who would grab on at the other end and step forward.

At the same time, the essay contest had a second half that targeted a separate audience: young Americans. In parallel to posing questions to young Middle Easterners about the pain of repression and deferred dreams for a better future, young Americans were asked to consider why they should care about the Mideast civil rights movement and how they could get involved as active supporters—without waiting for the US government. To address the silence of the "American street," questions challenged entrants on the American side of the contest to consider how to overcome the indifference of their peers to the civil rights realities of the Mideast, engage the region at a grassroots level, and build a transformative partnership with their liberal counterparts in the region.

While the best essays from that part of the contest were not included in this anthology, their spirit drives these concluding observations. You may not realize it, but you are vital to the success of the historic uprisings unfolding across the region. With your help, the deferred dreams of young Middle East-erners actually have a chance of becoming reality. Holding repressive lead-ers accountable and securing individual rights is no longer a fantasy for any Mideast country—but success will require a massive investment of outside support. We conclude therefore with a quick guide to how you can join the struggle.

INVISIBLE YOUNG DISSIDENTS MATTER: RECOGNIZE YOUR ALLIES

Despite the steep odds in 2005, the American Islamic Congress began seeking out the Middle East's neglected young dissidents for one simple reason: we sought partners on the ground to help advance individual rights. In a similar spirit, we ask you to consider the essayists in this anthology as allies in the struggle to advance liberal democracy in the region. First, because these young writers eloquently help improve our understanding of the Middle East's essential struggle as one for securing individual rights in the face of repressive forces. Second, because these thinkers are driving today's headline-grabbing events and shaping the region's future—and we need to appreciate where they are coming from to understand where they are headed. Finally, because their examples can inspire us to appreciate in new ways the power of our own freedom, calling us to action.

To be clear, the allies represented in the anthology do not necessarily advance comprehensive, liberal political agendas. A few explicitly would describe themselves as "liberals"—but other writers reject the liberal label. The region's autocrats and Islamists have managed, through a decades-long effort, to implement "no-fly zones" over the coordinates "liberal" and "democrat." Aversion to ideological programs is also partly a product of the essayists' age cohort. Few late teens or twenty-somethings anywhere in the world explicitly embrace liberalism as a complex political outlook.

Even so, the essayists affirm a set of liberal sensitivities. As the legendary literary critic Lionel Trilling observed, "the word liberal is a word primarily of political import, but its political meaning defines itself by the quality of life it envisages, by the sentiments it desires to affirm." The Sunni teenager in Iran humiliated for praying without a Shi'a *mohr* (prayer stone) may not be conversant with John Stewart Mill (or Lionel Trilling). Nevertheless, her basic call for justice—her desire for the Shi'a-majority state to respect her identity and individuality—is animated by liberal and democratic urges. Likewise, the Saudi student clashing with her Wahhabi Islamic studies teacher may frame her arguments in arcane theological terms, but she is ultimately making a stand for free inquiry and reasoned delibera-tion—the cornerstones of a liberal worldview.

The real conflict in the Middle East, then, is tied up in these writers' daily confrontations—not in the diplomatic dialogues held at dictators' pal-aces or the military confrontations that dominate Western coverage of the region. Recall that the popular uprisings engulfing the region were sparked by a young Tunisian street vendor humiliated by a policewoman's slap. One unknown young man's reaction to a personal indignity put an end to decades of repression and equally deceptive conventional wisdom.

That is why much of the essays' drama occurs in mundane settings: in public parks, during discussions on the subway, and even inside bedrooms. Perhaps the most common scene for encountering young Middle Easterners' dream deferred in this anthology is the classroom, with the teacher serving as a dictator stand-in and students as a public chorus reinforcing the exclusion and humiliation of the protagonist. The school campus offers a metaphor for the larger society and a stark backdrop against which the young dissident must stand out as a freethinking individual.

It is that individual on which the future of the Middle East hinges. Will these young men and women grow up free to define themselves as they want—or will their dreams be tied down by gender inequity and restrictions on free expression, ethnic minorities, and sexuality? Will the essayists spot-lighted in this anthology be able to speak their minds and express their com-plex identities in public without fear of political and physical repression? And will outsiders appreciate the stakes of the struggle and come to their aid?

For decades, no one living under a Middle Eastern dictatorship has en-joyed guaranteed civil rights. Basic freedoms are not recognized as natural rights, but instead as privileges granted or withdrawn at the whim of un-elected rulers. A dictator might choose to loosen restrictions—and then might just as quickly change his mind. Because no rights are guaranteed and because dictators constantly shift the red lines of acceptable conduct, the region's inhabitants have effectively been stripped of their individuality for decades. As one Moroccan essayist finds himself forced to admit, they are "subjects and not citizens."

What exploded out of Tunisia and burst across the Middle East was an instinctive movement for individual dignity led by young subjects who want to be treated as adult citizens. They are driven by a liberal sentiment that seeks recognition of popular rights and dignities. And regardless of the immediate outcome of these upheavals, the underlying challenge facing the region is whether the rights of the individual—of all individuals, including and especially ethnic, religious, and sexual minorities—will be guaranteed or instead remain subject to the whim of whoever dominates society.

This Middle Eastern conflict—between citizens and their rulers—may not be resolved for years, but it has already been indelibly shaped by the young thinkers featured in the anthology. Take, for example, Mohammed El-Dahshan, who submitted an essay in 2006 that dared to imagine Egypt as a liberal society with a free market, a female foreign minister, and no government censorship. At the time, his essay seemed a fantasy—almost science fiction—designed to offer an indirect condemnation of the status quo by sketching a better alternative. Yet he presciently set the essay in Cairo's Tahrir Square and, following the resignation of Hosni Mubarak, ran a piece in the *New York Times* reporting on how Mubarak's name and visage were being stripped from public buildings and landmarks. In other words, El-Dahshan was on to something—and when the moment of explosion came, he was in the thick of it.

So too was Dalia Ziada, the spunky young Egyptian whose provocative essay expressed her desire to transcend the constraints imposed upon her by "Mr. Society." Shortly after submitting her essay, Ziada would get the chance to do just that. Recruited to head the Egypt office of the American Islamic Congress, she set out to engage her generation in the struggle for individual rights. She published a comic book on Martin Luther King's Montgomery bus boycott, which would be distributed online and in hard copy (including in Tahrir Square), and launched the unprecedented Cairo Human Rights Film Festival to spotlight civil rights stories from around the world. Once a young writer motivated to submit an essay because of the prize money, she has now briefed the secretary of state and been dubbed by *Newsweek* as one of 150 women leaders "shaking the world."

By asking young social entrepreneurs to reflect on their deferred dreams, the essay contest purposely aimed to spark their activist spirit. That spirit is now unleashed in public and making waves across the region—and its impact is hardly limited to the Middle East. Indeed, the pain and the hope eloquently expressed in the preceding pages offer a call to action to anyone living in a free society. The essays underscore the degrading impact of political repression and the precious power of one's own freedoms, which need to be exercised to help support the struggle for individual rights in the region. This anthology can thus help us renew our own civic commitment to assisting the Middle East's indigenous young dissidents. The next essential step in that process is appreciating how we failed these dissidents for so long by allowing them to remain invisible.

LEARNING FROM PAST MISTAKES: WHY THE UPRISINGS CAUGHT THE WORLD BY SURPRISE

An old Mauritanian proverb cautions that "the shade will never be straight if the tree is crooked." In other words, our perception of reality can get distorted by faulty assumptions. In December 2010, as growing masses of Tunisians took to the streets to challenge repression, the two editors of this anthology saw a watershed moment. We met in a coffee shop and—between frenzied tweeting of breaking developments—penned an op-ed addressing the implications of the popular explosion. "Mideast autocrats like Tunisia's Ben Ali sit atop social pressure cookers they can no longer contain," we warned, calling for American policymakers to support the Tunisian people lest their revolution be hijacked by radical Islamists.

Both together and independently we had published numerous Mideast-related op-eds in prominent media outlets across the political spectrum, from the *Wall Street Journal* to the *Guardian*. Yet the response to the Tunisia opinion piece—including that from editors we had previously worked closely with—was dismissive. "Our readers would not be interested in Tunisia," wrote one. Others were skeptical that there was any significance behind the street demonstrations, as the grassroots struggle for civil rights in the region hardly registered on their radar screens. ("If it's not about the US or Israel, it's not news.")

When President Ben Ali was deposed by his own people a few days later, it came as a total shock to Western journalists, policymakers, and analysts who had long ignored young Mideast democrats and treated repression across the region as a backdrop to more pressing geopolitics. The failure to recognize dissidents resulted from a set of counterproductive thought patterns that the West has adopted in attempting to understand the Middle East. The result is a faulty narrative of the Middle East built atop the following pillars of conventional wisdom:

Headline Conflicts—For decades, the Middle East has been regarded primarily through the prism of the Arab-Israeli conflict and various Western military ventures in the region, most notably in Iraq. The obsession with these geopolitical challenges often became all-consuming for Western elites. Dictatorships were accepted as a natural part of the Mideast landscape, and the systematic repression of individual rights seemed such a quotidian fact of life that it hardly merited attention in the big game of shuttle diplomacy and "peace-processing." As a result, few stopped to take the pulse of what was going on beneath the surface or to consider the repressed energy of millions of young Middle Easterners with deferred dreams. Before 2011, Tunisia was a tourist destination where the PLO had its old headquarters; otherwise it was unremarkable and not of interest to American audiences.

Engagement—Every few years, "outreach to the Muslim world" was given priority status in the naïve hope that Mideast leaders would, in President Obama's words, "unclench their fists" and embrace cooperation. Regimes from the so-called resistance bloc (Iran, Syria, and Sudan) typically only clenched their fists tighter in response. Dictators closer to Washington and Brussels happily declared "reform" efforts that were in reality vapid public relations stunts posing no threat to entrenched power structures and alleged that the impending Islamist threat justified their "slow progress." Engaging the corrupt elites that misrule the so-called moderate regimes did not win hearts and minds, and engaging the totalitarian brutes of the resistance bloc only served to dishearten and isolate the democrats suffering beneath them.

In the anthology, the author of "Monologue with the Prince" experiences the charade of engagement firsthand. Though he resolves to press on for real change despite being snubbed by a "reformist" Saudi prince, his equally disillusioned friend reacts by becoming a suicide bomber in Iraq.

Non-Interventionism—To call for political freedom in the Mideast, went one common trope, meant imposing unwelcome Western values on the region's inhabitants and thus re-staging the trauma of colonialism. Underlying this argument was a kind of cultural relativism, most notoriously evoked by Egyptian Vice President Omar Suleiman in the dying days of the Mubarak regime: "We are not fully ready for democracy, which is not part of our culture and way of life." This falsehood had been internalized by some top Western policymakers. In the fall of 2010, as Bahrain cracked down on human rights activists, Assistant US Secretary of State for Near East Affairs Janet Sanderson visited the island nation and coolly declared: "We are not here, frankly, to impose our views on others, but to encourage the countries of the region to fulfill their priorities." Of course to tolerate abuses, as Yossi Klein Halevi has written, is an act of intervention—in favor of the oppressor. Consider, too, that moral and material support from the outside is a key element in civil rights campaigns imagined by several essayists in the anthology. Take, for instance, Raghda El-Halawany's proposed collaboration with the iconic American feminist group NOW to protect the rights of Egyptian woman. Alas, Raghda's dream remains largely a fantasy.

The "Authenticity" Fetish—Another intellectual roadblock, and a variation on the colonialism theme, was the suspicion that Mideast reformers are unrepresentative elites and thus somehow lack "authenticity." But young Middle Eastern liberals who are calling for gender equity, reproductive freedom, minority rights, and an end to homophobia deserve recognition. Moreover, the very notion of "authenticity" in the Middle East should be problematized. After centuries of conquest and contact with the outside world—not to mention recent technological advances connecting every corner of the region—there is no pristine Middle Eastern identity. The illustrator Omar Shukri who dares to express his atheism on TV—imagined in the essay by Tarek Shahin—is no less an authentic Middle Eastern character than the bearded cleric calling for violence in response to cartoons. In fact, just last October, a real world Shukri was thrust into the international spotlight: Bahadir Baruter, a Turkish editorial cartoonist, was charged by the Istanbul public prosecutor with "insulting the religious values adopted by part of the population" after he published a cartoon showing a mosque-goer chatting with God on his cellphone and asking to be pardoned from the last part of the prayer to run some errands. The cartoon contained a not-so-hidden message that read, "there is no Allah—religion is a lie." (As we write, Baruter faces a year in jail in nominally secular and democratic Turkey.)

Essentialization—A closely related intellectual stumbling block was the tendency to essentialize Muslims and Middle Easterners. A complex religion and a vast region were often reduced to the "Muslim world" in Western discourse. Where the region's inhabitants themselves located a wide range of cultural identities, including secular ones, Westerners saw a monolithic and often intolerant "Muslim identity." This approach transformed religion—personal beliefs that individuals accept, reject, and change over time—into an immutable character synonymous with race and ethnicity that could not be changed. The anthology's voices from a range of subcommunities and perspectives—the Sunni Iranian, the Amazigh Moroccan, the male feminist—counsel against the impulse to essentialize.

The Islamist Threat—Fears of an Islamist takeover also cooled Western enthusiasm for democratization and liberalization in the Middle East. The regional order was (and is) often seen as a zero-sum game in the conventional narrative: the region's autocrats form the only bulwarks against radical Islamists, and democratic openings ultimately only usher in theocratic regimes like Iran's Islamic Republic. These anxieties revealed themselves in some initial reactions to the popular uprisings in Tunisia and Egypt. Many observers saw a dreadful replay of the 1979 Islamic Revolution that swept the Ayatollah Khomeini to power—an impression only later deepened by the policies of Libyan rebels who overthrew Muammar Qaddafi and the electoral triumphs of Islamist parties in Tunisia and Egypt's post-revolutionary elections.

Radical Islamism is a paramount concern, for both the West and the Middle East. The region's liberal dissidents—including several essayists in the anthology—know firsthand the threat to freedom and human dignity that groups like the Muslim Brotherhood represent. But Islamists have often been the greatest indirect beneficiaries of Mideast autocrats, who, by suppressing every form of secular dissent, empowered Islamist groups as the only available channels for expressing dissent. For too long, the West clung to a rotten—and now rapidly disappearing—status quo, propping up or tolerating a region dominated almost entirely by dictators who stunted, nearly fatally, attempts to cultivate viable liberal movements in the Middle East.

The Islamists' recent electoral success in countries like Tunisia and Egypt should be seen not as a vindication of their ideologies per se, but as a testament to their internal organizational capabilities—and as a warning of the vulnerability of liberals, who have emerged from dictatorships without the support needed to build comparable networks and strategies. Today on the ground in the region there is battle of "to-dos" on very practical terms: Who can you recruit? How large a network can you build? Which institutions can advance your message in an open market of ideas? Thanks in part to petrol-patrons from the Gulf, Islamists have deep pockets, wide support networks, and massive media artillery. Liberals, by contrast, have obscure intellectual websites and small grants from a few Western embassies and foundations. Observers at many polling stations during Tunisia's historic October 2011 elections, for example, noted that only the Islamist Ennahda Party had representatives on hand throughout the day. While the Islamists ran a disciplined grassroots campaign over many months, liberal parties remained disorganized and only began campaigning in earnest a few weeks prior to the election.

Intra-Islamist solidarity—financial, ideological, media, moral, and logistical—has been a key strength in fueling the movement's survival and rise. Yet just because the Islamists are scoring tactical victories does not absolve the West from fulfilling its moral duty to stand with its ideological allies: the liberals, feminists, and secularists. Too much energy is dissipated in hand-wringing over an Islamist challenge that has been clear for decades. Admonitions and warning bells without solutions ring hollow and are of no practical use to the already embattled liberals. Crying about an Islamist takeover has no practical ramification for fending off the threat itself, aside perhaps from embracing the unsustainable panacea of keeping a strongman in power. This sad state of affairs shows a lack of imagination and a less than generous spirit. Indeed, the fact that the essays in this anthology seem so unusual to Western readers is reflective of the failure to engage and elevate liberal and secular voices in a much more robust and effective way during the past decades.

Today, there remains a historic opening. For the first time in decades there is space to mount counter-solutions to the Manichean choice of autocrat or Islamist. The current revolutionary tide is a once-in-a-generation opportunity, as Islamists were neither the precursors nor the triggers of the uprising, and Islamists have much to lose in a new open society that allows dissident voices to speak freely. In essence, the region's liberals need an ideological Marshall Plan. Just as the West invested in Europe to fend off communism, the Middle East deserves now more than ever high levels of energy and strategic planning to fend off Islamism. Otherwise, just as countries like Czechoslovakia were lost to communism for decades, so too the newly liberated states in North Africa and beyond may succumb to Islamist obscurantism for a generation or more.

The focus, then, should be on seeking positive opportunities wherever we find them—and particularly on assisting young Middle Easterners in their quest to become entrepreneurs of their own destinies. The long-term goal should be the emergence of free societies, based on individual rights, where there once stood the world's least free region. To achieve this vision, we need a blueprint for moving beyond the failed paradigms of the past and empowering the Mideast's nascent civil rights movement to shape the future.

GET IN GEAR: START DREAMING

The uprisings sweeping the Middle East have at last forced a reckoning with the old failed narrative of the region. More importantly, the crumbling old order has created an opening for one of the most important actors in the fight for Mideast liberalism: you. As a citizen of a free society, you can play a powerful role in extending the rights we enjoy to those fated to be born under dictatorship. Put another way, your apathy has been a strategic asset for Middle Eastern dictators.

To start, you have to get over any hang-ups about your role as an outsider. Remember that the indispensability of outside support—including financial—and the backlash against it are by no means unique to the Middle East. The American civil rights movement itself would have failed without the assistance of free people from outside the South. In 1956, for instance, white kindergarteners at a Wisconsin church sent their Sunday collection to the Montgomery bus boycotters. Too young to write letters, they sent along drawings, which Martin Luther King displayed to activists. Another outsider, Bayard Rustin, came down to Alabama from Pennsylvania to help the bus boycotters by encouraging them to voluntarily flood Montgomery's jails and in turn securing emergency bail money from wealthy white New Yorkers. He then organized a fundraiser in New York, packing 18,000 cheering supporters into Madison Square Garden to hear Eleanor Roosevelt and Sammy Davis Jr. and raise thousands of dollars for Montgomery.

As more and more Americans began to wake up to the daily injustices inflicted on southern blacks, hundreds of northern students, ministers and rabbis, and other average citizens took Freedom Rides to regions they had never before visited. Their activism is, in retrospect, all the more remarkable because at the time few appreciated that being a bystander effectively meant tolerating intolerance. Just as some argue today in the Middle East, back in the day, de jure apartheid in the American South was viewed as an "authentic" culture and the intrusion of young northern "outsiders" was an offensive imposition of foreign values. The South, after all, was still smarting from northern domination and "colonialism" since the end of the Civil War in 1865.

Even Dr. King himself was attacked as an outsider. When he moved his protest focus to the city of Birmingham, white leaders and even a few local black community elders denounced his intrusion into their city's politics—not unlike the way dictators condemn local dissidents and their allies in the international human rights community as part of an American conspiracy. "I challenged those who had been persuaded I was an 'outsider,'" King later wrote. "I expanded further on the weary and worn 'outsider' charge, which we have faced in every community where we have gone to try to help. No Negro, in fact, no American is an outsider when he goes to any community to aid the cause of freedom and justice."

There is an underground scene of Americans—from both sides of aisle—who have already heeded King's admonition and stepped up to help inspire and support Mideast reformers. Ethan Zuckerman, a hi-tech entrepreneur, saw the opportunity to enable a global conversation unfettered by censorship and language divides. With former CNN journalist Rebecca MacKinnon, he launched Global Voices as a network of bloggers from the around the world. When members of the network began facing political harassment and arrest, Global Voices brought on Sami Ben Gharbia, one of Tunisia's top cyber-dissidents, to organize grassroots advocacy efforts for online free speech worldwide and a solidarity base for jailed dissidents. Ben Gharbia and his team at Nawaat.org would go on to play a key role in distributing to the world news from Tunisia's uprising and in turn pumping support back to the grassroots protestors.

You don't have to be an international tech mogul to make an impact. Take Jane Novak, a New Jersey stay-at-home mom with no Arabic skills or Mideast travel experience who managed to single-handedly become the number one foreign nemesis of the Yemeni regime. Novak's living room hardly seems the ideal spot for leading a civil rights revolution, yet the mother of two became a household name for many Yemenis simply by writing at her computer. Blocked inside Yemen, her blog "Armies of Liberation"—with an American flag at the top and a quote from Franklin Roosevelt—systematically and tirelessly chronicles police brutality and abuses of women and the press in Yemen.

Novak's interest in Yemen began when she read a small article about the imprisonment of journalist Abdulkarim al-Khaiwani in 2004. Determined to awaken Westerners to his plight, she wrote five articles and circulated them worldwide. A young Yemeni journalist named Sami No'aman discovered and translated them into Arabic for a local newspaper. This in turn earned her a guest appearance on Al Jazeera Arabic alongside a Yemeni government official, who was flustered by Novak's courage in speaking truth to his illegitimate power. He began yelling at her live on air. But Novak's persistence paid off, and al-Khaiwani was soon granted amnesty.

"I learned about the enormous challenges Yemeni journalists face," Novak told us. "I came to deeply respect them as modern heroes. People with rights have an obligation to work for the people who don't. Other people can become informed and bring pressure on the American government to live up to its founding ideals." Jane Novak is looking for a few good men and women.

Now it's your turn to start dreaming. Tap into the daring, imaginative streak displayed by the anthology's essayists and their Western supporters like Ethan Zuckerman and Jane Novak. Think of simple or transformative campaigns you could help inspire. Here are a few deferred dreams to spark your own creativity:

Dictatorship Studies—Part of the reason Americans failed to anticipate the 2011 Arab uprisings and the 2009 wave of protest in Iran was a poor understanding of how dictatorships work and their impact on ordinary citizens. But a new student movement pressures universities to introduce a minor on dictatorship. Enterprising young academics publish informative new books analyzing the social impact of civil rights repression in the Mideast. To enhance the curriculum, filmmakers produce provocative YouTube documentary series that bring the challenge home in full color. (In fact, the American Islamic Congress is launching a new version of the Dream Deferred contest, this time to entice young viral video makers to create visually compelling testaments of the value of the civil rights struggle—in a retort to the obscene martyrdom videos popularized by al-Qaeda.)

Target the Dictators' US Outposts—In a dramatic reversal of the Islamic Revolution in Iran, when activists stormed the US Embassy and took hundreds of hostages, hundreds of American students of diverse backgrounds and political views converge around the regime's mission to the United Nations in New York, haranguing diplomats to release the leaders of the Green Movement and other dissidents. The mission—along with the Iranian Interests Section in Washington—is swamped, and bureaucrats send frantic cables back to Tehran demanding action to alleviate the pressure. (Or join Jane Novak outside the Yemeni consulate.)

The Persian Gulf International Labor Campaign—The millions of non-Arab migrant workers, who constitute the overwhelming majority of the populations in many Gulf states, achieve labor standards for the first time, thanks to a mobilization spearheaded by grassroots activists with support from the AFL-CIO. Union recruiters from around the world crisscross the region, enlisting new members at factories and evening community meetings. With their ranks newly swelling, unions become a powerful force in the domestic politics of Qatar, Kuwait, and the UAE, successfully agitating for fair wages and prosecution of abusive employers.

The Benghazi Concert for Human Freedom—While Libya's cultural offerings were once confined to a few bookstores dedicated to Colonel Qaddafi's insane, four-volume *Green Book* manifesto, Benghazi hosts the annual Middle East Concert for Human Freedom. Leading regional musicians share the stage for a show broadcast on satellite TV and streamed live to a global Internet audience. Performers call on political leaders to adopt a bill of basic rights protecting individual freedoms. Bruce Springsteen makes a cameo appearance for an all-star rendition of Bob Dylan's "Blowing in the Wind," with verses translated into Persian, Arabic, and Tamazight. Funds raised go toward a legal defense fund for political dissidents that remain imprisoned throughout the region.

The Road to Damascus Alternative Book Fair—Ammar Abdulhamid's Dar Emar publishing house hosts the Middle East's largest progressive book fair in Damascus's Old Quarter. Translations of *The Diary of Anne Frank,* Martin Luther King's *Letters from a Birmingham Jail,* William S. Burroughs's *Naked Lunch,* and even Frederick Hayek's *The Road to Serfdom* are snatched up by eager crowds. Holocaust survivor and Nobel Peace Prize winner Elie Wiesel moderates a panel featuring the poet Maya Angelou and *Vagina Monologues* playwright Eve Ensler. Prizes for poetry and prose are handed out to Syrian high school and college students.

Mecca Interfaith Conference—After centuries of banning all non-Muslims, the epicenter of the "Muslim world" throws its doors open for an ambitious symposium on interfaith dialogue. Rabbis and ministers tour archaeological sites of seventh-century Jewish and Christian communities. Hindu, Buddhist, and Shinto clerics, too, all mingle in the plaza outside the Kaba, and some even join a guided tour through the ornate sanctuary. Added bonus: all participants are ferried to the conference by female cabbies.

Tehran University's Salman Rushdie Prize for Literature—On the campus where ayatollahs once condemned a novelist (and his publishers and translators) to death over a work of fiction now comes a new top literature prize celebrating authors who challenge boundaries to broaden human understanding. The annual award ceremony follows a weeklong seminar dedicated to analyzing once-banned books.

After you have fun dreaming up fantasies like these, the third and most important step is to identify the practical steps that might one day lead to their becoming reality. A Rushdie Prize at an Iranian university—or a gay pride parade through downtown Riyadh—may never come to be. Yet not long ago the idea that a group of young activists dedicated to nonviolence could bring down Hosni Mubarak, a pharaoh presiding over the capital with the most security officials per capita in the world, sounded like a wild fantasy. Nor would the prospect of a free Tripoli have seemed even remotely within the realm of possibility. The dream deferred often seems to falter or recede, but that never means it cannot burst forth.

If nothing else, recent events in the Middle East are a reminder that no system is set in stone and that radical change can be simply a day away. The challenge for you is to dream big and then start small with basic, practical steps, harnessing new technology and new opportunities while applying timeless lessons from past successful movements for human freedom. A few practical tips include:

- Stay informed by subscribing to the American Islamic Congress's e-newsletter *The CRIME Report*. The acronym stands for "Civil Rights in the Middle East" and offers a reminder that advocating for basic rights often lands Middle Easterners in jail. As a briefing on alleged "crimes," the newsletter spotlights the region's expanding civil rights movement with edgy wit and opportunities to become "partners in crime" with grassroots reformers. See http://www.hamsaweb.org/crime.

- If you're more of an intellectual than an activist, seize opportunities to challenge reigning orthodoxies about the region. Armed with the narratives shared in this anthology, you no longer have to accept, say, a Middle East Studies professor's claims that human rights advocacy in the region amounts to "cultural imperialism" or "neo-colonialism." Thus, the voices gathered here can serve as powerful salvos in Mideast-related policy and philosophical debates in the West.

- Or enter the American half of the Dream Deferred Essay Contest. You get a forum to share creative ideas for assisting civil rights reform along with the chance to win thousands of dollars in prizes. Crafting your essay is a great way to think through a concrete plan to help. See http://www.hamsaweb.org/essay.

- See your smartphone as a nonviolent weapon. Your phone is an always-on access point to viral videos, Twitter alerts, and email updates from activists in the region. In addition to consuming cutting-edge content from the region, you can help spread the word via your own social media feeds. Simply sharing updates with your friends and followers helps deepen the impact of grassroots efforts in the region. Plus you can tweet back, offering encouragement and insights. We have developed several close friendships with activists in the region we have never met in person—and the online collaboration has helped us better understand the region and helped them be more effective in their activism.

Beyond these basic steps, start thinking ahead to the next tier of explosions that are not yet on the world's radar screen. For instance, as noted above, many Gulf states are filled with a quasi-slave class of millions of non-citizen workers who have no opportunity for social advancement while carrying out all these countries' manual labor. This time bomb has not yet been activated nor has it received substantial international coverage. Identifying emerging challenges like these gives you the opportunity to do cutting-edge work today on tomorrow's headlines.

When it comes to the world's least free region, dreaming is perhaps the most realistic approach. So many political and social movements have been tried and failed. So much destruction and stagnation have scarred the Middle East. For too long, artificial barriers, largely of our own creation, have inhibited us from imagining what a free Middle East could look like. The essays in this anthology offer an accounting of the enormous human cost of repression and abdication—as well as the potential payoff that could come with genuine democratization and liberalization.

Now that popular uprisings have suddenly shattered illusions of stability and upended decades-old dictatorships, the need to translate dreams into reality is all the more pressing. The Middle East is up for grabs as never before, and the real struggle for civil rights has just entered a critical new phase. For all the wonder of watching dictators laid low by nonviolent protestors, there is no guarantee that what comes next is open societies that recognize the individual rights of their diverse citizens. Indeed, Islamist radicals and old-guard elites remain daunting threats to the emergence of genuine freedom—and the energy of entrepreneurial liberal dissidents and their Western supporters is more critical than ever.

Whether our motivation is the price of gasoline, the national security threat of terrorism, or the morally inspiring struggle for individual rights in the face of brutal dictatorship, we all have a stake. Americans—particularly members of the emerging generation who grew up in the wake of September 11 and amid the social media revolution—need to recognize that standing up for civil rights in the Middle East is not about right or left, but right and wrong. If we can organize effectively, the results can be transformative. As the outcome of the Arab Spring hangs in the balance between democracy, theocracy, and dictatorship, the dream of a liberal awakening in the Middle East can no longer be deferred.

COEDITORS

NASSER WEDDADY

A native of Mauritania, Weddady grew up in Libya and Syria, traveling extensively through the Middle East as the privileged son of a diplomat. As a young man, he met leaders like Muammar Qaddafi, Hafez al-Assad, and Yasser Arafat and saw firsthand the toll dictatorship and civil rights repression were taking on the region. He also witnessed black slavery in Mauritania, an experience that ultimately shocked him into becoming an abolitionist and human rights advocate. Because of his outspoken work, Weddady fled to the United States as a refugee in 2000. Then, a few days after the September 11 attacks, he was mistakenly detained by the FBI because of his appearance.

Today, Weddady is the civil rights outreach director of the American Islamic Congress. He helped design and administer the Dream Deferred Essay Contest, and he has organized workshops for essay contest winners across the Middle East. Several of the essay contest participants have themselves faced repression for their outspoken work, and Weddady has consequently helped lead several high-profile campaigns (mostly successful) to free imprisoned dissidents in North Africa, Bahrain, Egypt, Yemen, Saudi Arabia, Iran, and beyond.

Fluent in five languages (including Hebrew), Weddady has published in the *International Herald Tribune,* the *Wall Street Journal,* the *Boston Globe,* the *Baltimore Sun,* and the *Daily Beast;* appeared on CNN, FOX News, BBC World Service, Al Jazeera, and Radio Liberty; and testified before Congress. He has lectured at the United States Institute of Peace, the Equal Employment Opportunity Commission, and in challenging interfaith settings. His Twitter feed (@weddady) is widely followed by activists and journalists around the world, and he is currently ranked among Boston's most influential Twitter users.

SOHRAB AHMARI

Born in Tehran, Ahmari experienced life under the repressive Iranian regime first-hand, including being interrogated by security officials as a child about his parents and facing disciplinary action for accidentally bringing a *Star Wars* Betamax video to school (Western films were officially banned in Iran at the time), before emigrating to the United States as a teenager.

An alumnus of Teach for America, Ahmari today studies law at Northeastern University. Fluent in Persian, he frequently addresses diverse audiences about the struggle for individual liberty in the Middle East. A *Huffington Post* blogger, Ahmari's columns, feature stories, and book reviews have appeared in prominent print and online venues across the political spectrum, including the *Guardian*, the New York *Daily News*, the *Boston Globe*, the *Chronicle of Higher Education*, the *National Post* (Canada), the *New Republic*, the *Weekly Standard*, *Commentary*, *Dissent*, *City Journal*, and *World Affairs*, among others.

ACKNOWLEDGMENTS

THIS BOOK NEVER WOULD HAVE EXISTED WITHOUT THE VISION and support of Zainab Al-Suwaij, the co-founder and executive director of the American Islamic Congress. Had an anthology like this been published two decades ago, Zainab would no doubt have written one of the outstanding essays. A budding poet and the granddaughter of Basra's leading ayatollah, she grew up under Saddam Hussein with the dream deferred of a better life in freedom. In 1991, she acted on that dream and rose up with many fellow Iraqis in a remarkable but ultimately futile attempt to liberate Iraq. For a brief week, she witnessed much of Iraq liberated from Saddam's rule, including torture chambers thrown open and communities organizing without the dreaded *mukhabarat* (internal security forces) to oppress them. But the promised American aid never came, Saddam regrouped, and the uprising collapsed. After burning much of her poetry and her diary, Zainab went into hiding and then fled her homeland. She came to the United States to rebuild her life but never forgot her dream deferred.

After the September 11 attacks, Zainab saw the need for responsible Muslim-American leadership and created the American Islamic Congress. In 2005, she was instrumental in supporting and raising funds for the launch of Dream Deferred Essay Contest, as well as its promotion throughout the Middle East. She has served as a judge for the essay contest, recruited other celebrity judges, and continued to inspire young contest winners to act in pursuit of their dreams. It was with her encouragement that we pursued this anthology, and it is her leadership that everyday strengthens the American Islamic Congress as a unique and vital civil rights organization promoting responsible leadership in the United States and around the world.

The anthology also would not have come into being without the team at Palgrave Macmillan, especially Emily Carleton, who took a chance on our proposal, and Laura Lancaster, Victoria Wallis, and Georgia Maas, who closely supported us throughout the publishing process.

The spark behind the anthology was, of course, the essay contest. Thousands of young thinkers were inspired to enter the contest in part because of the $10,000 in prizes awarded each year. The Earhart Foundation has helped underwrite those prizes year after year. Special recognition is due to the Foundation's board, which took a risk on the concept and continued to provide support as it grew over the years. Thanks also to the Foundation's president, Dr. Ingrid A. Gregg, and secretary, Montgomery B. Brown.

Every year, cash prizes were supplemented by fifty book prizes, generously donated by the Liberty Fund. Chris Talley, president of the Liberty Fund, kindly coordinated each donation. The Unitarian Universalist Service Committee also helped support efforts to publicize the contest and engage its winners in training conferences. The UUSC's Wayne Smith played a critical role and even served as a judge for the contest. His colleagues Fatema Haji-Taki, Anna Bartlett, Atema Eclai, and Martha Thompson all helped continue and deepen UUSC's support for AIC's civil rights work. Another key element in encouraging young thinkers to enter the contest were the prominent personalities who volunteered to serve as "celebrity judges." Over the essay contest's history, a diverse group of individuals have kindly lent their names to the contest and provided critical feedback on finalist essays. Thanks to Khaled Abol Naga, Ahmed Ahmed, Abdulkarim al-Khaiwani, Mahmood Al-Yousif, Dr. Rola Dashti, Mona Eltahawy, Dr. Shafeeq Ghabra, Roya Hakakian, Rana Husseini, Dr. Saad Eddin Ibrahim, Lily Mazahery, Parisa Montazaran, Dr. Azar Nafisi, Dean Obeidallah, and Abdel Nasser Ould Yessa.

We owe a special debt of gratitude to several judges for the outstanding roles they played. Syrian dissident Ammar Abdulhamid directly inspired the contest with his musing about the need for an essay competition with cash prizes to encourage young liberals to share their dreams. Dr. Tom G. Palmer of the CATO Institute played a critical role in making introductions to the Earhart Foundation and the Liberty Fund and helping mentor outstanding winners from the contest. Tom's passion for promoting liberty on the grassroots level is infectious. In addition, Ahmed Benchemsi, a long-serving judge and founder of Morocco's best-selling weekly magazine *TelQuel*, brought a particular passion to the task of reviewing finalist essays. As described in more detail in the preceding pages, Ahmed was so excited by one essay that he had it translated into French and run in a special edition of *TelQuel.* And then there is Gloria Steinem, who served as an inaugural judge for the essay contest and kindly contributed the foreword to this anthology. We are also grateful to President Lech Walesa for his support of the book. His life's work is an inspiration.

Many current and former staff and interns at AIC helped advance the essay contest from idea to launch to an annual institution. Special thanks to Lauren Murphy for years of hard work helping to coordinate so many of the contest's administrative aspects—and to Dalia Ziada for translation and promotion work on the ground in Egypt. Vera Koshkina helped launch the contest, and Anne Willborn helped prepare the initial proposal for this anthology. Colleagues and interns who provided assistance include Abdel Maliky, Jill Holcomb, Shakir Mohammed, Jeehan S. B. Faiz, Bashir Martin, Andrea Dettorre, Dina Abkairova, Krupa Vithlani, Mohammed Harba, Mourad Afani, Jihath Goznavi, Denia Hasic, Sarah Sadiq, Kseniya Zudava, Clark Hayes, Javed Rezayee, Chris Whyte, Erum Rahman, Emmanuel Benhamou, Katrina Timlin, Farah Mohamed, Allyson Junker, Sana Alikalyan, Anas Qtiesh, Cybele Safadi, Sana Nasir, Doug Helman, Carolyn Brunelle, Davina Abujudeh, Arsla Jawid, Phil Hoffman, Rebecca Rogers, Richard Chen, Rohit Biswas, Kelly Dalla Tezza, Khalid Ben Khalid, Marie Gagnon, Subrina Hudson, Hena Haidari, Liz Jameson, and Celia Richa

Thanks also to the many people who have supported, mentored, and encouraged us, including: Zamzam Syed, Jamal Ait Hammou, Raza Shaikh, Addi Ouadderrou, Zaur Mamedov, Afrah Farah, Ala Khaki, Adnan Zubcevic, Serap Kantarci, Fatai Illupeju, Mehmet Ali Sanlikol, Farha Hasan, Djamal Bekkai, Fallou Ngom, Alex Zito, Shahla Haeri, Ali Asani, Saima Firdoos, Nadira Bijan, Jumana Dahodwala, Mohamed Eljahmi, Salameh Nematt, Samuel Tadros, Akbar Atri, Rob Leikind, Giovanna Negretti, Comy and Peter Kohanloo, Ali Salimi, Ebi and Arya Shams, Bijan Mehr, Stephen Hull, Abdullah al-Qubati, Thor Halvorssen, Alex Gladstein, Caitlin Rosengarten, Amira Maaty, Angela Wu, Tina Ramirez, Marco Greenberg, Blake Parker, Dafna Rand, David Gerzof, Lina Ben Mhenni, Lorenzo Vidino, Peter Ackerman, Roba al-Assi, Brad Lips, Sajid Anani, Armineh Johannes, Haleh Esfandiari, Leila Austin, Jad Madi, Latifa Akharbach, Sami Noaman, Alaa Abdelfatah, Slim Amamou, Fares Mabrouk, Jane Novak, Dianne Sehler, Ladan Boroumond, Azucena Rodriguez, Ethan Zuckerman, Golnaz Esfandiari, Munir Mawari, Raquel Evita, Sami Ben Gharbia, Steve Riskin, Fouad al-Farhan, Hanevy Ould Daha, Jay McAlly, and Usama Najeeb. Many thanks to Ben Cohen for reviewing early drafts of the introduction and conclusion, and to Michael Yon for donating photographs.

Sohrab Ahmari would like to thank the many editors who took chances on his writing over the years, including: Marjorie Pritchard at the *Boston Globe;* Joshua Greenman at the New York *Daily News;* Brian Whitaker at the *Guard-*

ian; Nick Sabloff at the *Huffington Post;* Isaac Chotiner at the *New Republic;* Karen Winkler at the *Chronicle of Higher Education;* Kelly McParland at the *National Post;* John Podhoretz and Abe Greenwald at *Commentary;* Richard Starr, Lee Smith, and Daniel Halper at the *Weekly Standard;* Michael Walzer, Michael Kazin, Maxine Phillips, and Nick Serpe at *Dissent;* James Denton, Andrew Ivers, and Peter Collier at *World Affairs;* Brian Anderson, Ben Plotinsky, and Paul Beston at *City Journal;* and Jordan Fabian at *The Hill.* He would also like to thank James Kirchick for opening countless doors; Dean Emily Spieler and Professors David Phillips and Daniel Austin of the Northeastern University School of Law for their support; and Leon Wieseltier for years of inspiration: "One should not wish to be influenced; one should wish to be convinced."

We must also recognize all the writers who entered the essay contest and in particular those whose writing comprises the heart of this book. A few of the essay entrants have spent time or are currently in jail because of their writings, including Kareem Amer and Maikel Nabil Sanad. Precisely because speaking publicly carries such risks, many entrants have requested anonymity—but just because their full names cannot appear in print does not in any way negate the power of their writing.

Finally, we want to thank all the supporters of the American Islamic Congress. AIC is a civil rights organization dedicated to promoting tolerance and the exchange of ideas among Muslims and between all peoples. Its diverse members are part of a vital effort to rally people "passionate about moderation." If you are not already a member, visit http://www.aicongress.org to learn how you can get involved.

INDEX